TELL ME YOU'RE

TELL ME YOU'RE SORRY, DADDY

Two scared little girls.
One abusive father.
One survived against all odds
to tell their story.

Caryn Walker

with Linda Watson-Brown

JOHN BLAKE

First published in Great Britain by John Blake Publishing,
an imprint of Kings Road Publishing
Suite 2.25 The Plaza
535 Kings Road
London SW10 0SZ

www.johnblakebooks.com

www.facebook.com/johnblakebooks
twitter.com/jblakebooks

First published in paperback in 2018

ISBN: 978 1 78606 876 7
Ebook 978-1-78606-918-4

British Library Cataloguing-in-Publication Data:
A catalogue record for this book is available from the British Library.

Design by www.envydesign.co.uk

Printed and bound in Great Britain by Clays Ltd, Elcograf S p. A

1 3 5 7 9 10 8 6 4 2

© Text copyright Caryn Walker 2018

The right of Caryn Walker to be identified as the author of this work
has been asserted by her in accordance with the Copyright, Designs and
Patents Act 1988.

Papers used by John Blake Publishing are natural, recyclable products made from
wood grown in sustainable forests. The manufacturing processes conform to the
environmental regulations of the country of origin.

Every attempt has been made to contact the relevant copyright-holders,
but some were unobtainable. We would be grateful if the appropriate people
could contact us.

Dedicated to my sister, Jenny – this book will give you the voice you never had.

And for all the victims of childhood abuse – I hope this gives you the courage to come forward and speak up.

CONTENTS

PROLOGUE

Dear Jenny

This is going to be hard. I won't pretend anything other than that – I am trying to put together the story of our lives and I know there will be times when I won't even be sure that I'm doing the right thing. I'm surrounded by files and notes and records, but I'm also surrounded by ghosts and memories and heartache. I won't get through this without a lot of tears, but I know, no matter how many I shed, they will never bring you back; they will never make up for what was done to you.

But I watched them. I watched them for years, Jenny. I saw what they did to you, how they made you hate yourself, made you think you were worthless. I knew our dad abused you and I knew our mother made you feel as if you were nothing. I was just a little girl, just the little sister – and it was happening to me too. I saw it all, Jenny, and I lived it all. For so long I was helpless – unable to act, unable to get myself out of it, and at the mercy of people who should have done something to break up our toxic family.

There was nothing I could do, Jenny . . .

. . . until I could do something.

What they all forgot was that little sisters grow up. Scared girls, abused daughters, watchful siblings – they grow up. And they never forget. I made a promise to you and it's time for me to keep that promise. I'll make them pay. I'll make them pay for what they did to you, Jenny. There will be a price for me too, I know that, but I don't care. After all, it can never be as steep as the one you paid.

So, I'll try to write it – my story, your story, our story – but who knows where this will take us? I am uncovering things all the time. The folders and bits of paper that make up our lives, the parts that were recorded by other people. They didn't know the half of it. It's time for me to put it all together, and to do justice to your memory.

There will be horrors here, but it all comes from a place of love. My love for you: the big sister who isn't here to help me through this; the big sister I will always remember. There are so many like us, an army of the broken and the abused; we exist in numbers that would shock the world if anyone paid attention to the lives of horror so many children experience; but we have a strength inside, a core of steel that makes us survive and makes us soar above it all once we finally realise *it was never our fault.* None of this was your fault, Jenny; none of this was my fault. We asked for none of it, and we each had to get through it in the best way we could. Our endings may have been different, but we are bound for ever, and I want the world to know your name. To acknowledge that you mattered.

Some people say that our stories are written in the stars, others that we make our own fortune. I'm not sure what to believe, because part of me feels that we were doomed from the moment we were born, but part of me thinks that you can always fight, you can always try to make the life you deserve, even when the universe has seemingly done all it possibly can to stop that from happening. Which one was it for us, Jenny? That's what I'm trying to work out. The only thing that is certain is my love for you and my belief that we all deserve a chance to break free from the lottery of our birth. I love you, Jenny – and I'll need *your* love to get me through this. I'll be back to share our story with you. I'll be back to take your hand as we go through this together.

Are you ready? This is where our 'once upon a time' begins . . .

Your little sister, Caryn xx

CHAPTER 1

TOXIC
1970

Mum had a life before she met Dad. Everyone does, of course, but sometimes it doesn't matter. Some people plod along through life, some people manage to stay within the lines; my mother wasn't 'some people'. It hadn't been a spectacular life – she didn't have an amazing career or a talent that stopped people in their tracks – but there was a history there, a back story, which would impact on everything that happened to me and my sister.

Mum was born into a very normal family. Her father, Bert, had been in the Navy, and her mother, Ivy, had her own seamstress shop. They were good, solid people. They had a neat, tidy house that was always clean as a new pin. They were upstanding neighbours, working-class, decent, respectable and reliable. They believed you should never get into debt, and that hard work was its own reward. They were the type of people who have been the backbone of this country for years. But times were changing, and those changes would be beyond anything they could ever have imagined.

Ivy and Bert had two little boys called Philip and Peter, and a girl called Jeanette. They were happy, settled, straightforward – and they also had Mum. Born a few years after World War Two had ended, their first child, she should have been the apple of their eye. Instead, as Nanny Ivy would later tell me, 'Our Lesley was born bad.'

The older I got, the more I heard these things. 'Lesley was a naughty child from the get-go,' Nanny would say with a sigh. 'She came home from school on her first day with a big grin on her face. I hoped they'd been able to tame her and she would be happy with the structure of being at school, but no – she was delighted with herself that she'd been in trouble from the moment she got there and made the teacher's life a misery.' Nanny had a saying she often used about Mum – 'She was on the clock from day one.' It did seem that Mum just enjoyed being naughty, and while as a child she might have been no more than infuriating to others, she took it into her teenage years and beyond, where it went well into the realms of danger and upset.

Nanny always said that Mum seemed happy when she reported that the teachers were at the end of their tether or that she'd got into trouble yet again. She loved attention and didn't care how she got it.

It wasn't only outside home that she caused friction. Auntie Jeanette was epileptic and, as such, probably did command a bit of extra attention from Nanny Ivy – rightly so – but Mum acted out against this and, when they were children, was caught pushing her vulnerable little sister downstairs on more than one occasion. When challenged, she would either just deny things – even when it was perfectly obvious that she was the guilty party – or smile. Both responses infuriated Nanny Ivy and, even years later, she would always mention Mum's 'nasty streak'.

'That girl has a side to her that no one realises,' she would say. 'She'd start a fight in an empty room, and she cares for no one but herself.'

I'm getting ahead of myself here but family histories are funny things. They start before you come into the picture, before anyone has even thought of you, but it all matters; it all affects how you'll be and how your story will turn out. There are foundations laid, there are tendencies that are nurtured or denied, there are slights that people carry with them forever, and there are tales that get passed down from generation to generation. I read something once that said we all have a particular role to play in any given relationship; and it's not as simple as just being wife, mother, daughter, sister, friend. It's more about how people expect us to act within those roles, and the behaviour we bring to each relationship. I think many of us feel that keenly, and we often fall into a trap of being less than true to ourselves in some relationships or friendships, as the other party expects us to be the friend who never complains, or the partner who always reacts, or the person who is a martyr. When we finally recognise that, we can move out of unhealthy behaviours and start to be our authentic self; but my sense of Mum, from the many stories I've been told, as well as witnessing her behaviour at first hand for years, is that she was never one to bow down to other people's expectations and she always did what she wanted; and she broke her parents' hearts in the process.

Mum turned from a naughty little girl into an uncontrollable teenager. Ivy and Bert despaired of their eldest and became almost resigned to the tales that would reach their ears. Lesley was mixing with a bad crowd, she was too fond of boys, she was running wild. Neighbours gossiped that she was involved with a married man and, before long – almost inevitably – they were faced with scandalous news: their unmarried daughter was pregnant. Such a thing was still seen as shameful. The permissive sixties were not all that the history books would have us believe. Young, unwed, working-class women who became pregnant after unprotected sex with married men were hardly welcomed by their families or their communities. My grandparents were distraught, wondering where they had gone wrong and what they could have done differently with this one daughter. From what I've been able to piece together, Mum's lover had no intention of leaving his wife for the teenager who thought he was her ticket to getting out of the life she found so boring. The birth of my half-brother, Ian, did nothing to change his mind. Nanny Ivy and Granddad Bert decided they would do all they could and supported their daughter. With the disapproval of neighbours and other family members very obvious, they – once again – stood by their child and looked after the new baby. They should have known that a leopard doesn't change its spots. Mum acted as if it was only right that they should take on the responsibility of baby Ian, while she used the time to meet up with her boyfriend whenever she could.

I have no idea whether Mum thought she could change his mind by getting pregnant again, but she went for that option anyway. She was only twenty when she conceived my half-sister, Jennifer, and it made absolutely no difference whatsoever to her relationship with the father. Her married boyfriend still refused to leave his wife – in fact, he told her that he wanted nothing to do with her or their children ever again.

At that point, Mum's luck changed – whether by accident or design, she met Norman Yeo. He didn't seem to mind that she was pregnant with another man's child, or that she already had a young baby, as he proposed after only a few months of courting. That would set the scene for much of their relationship – impulsive and with no thought of consequences.

Dad was an only child and his parents had always wanted 'their Norman' to have a special wedding day. It was to be the first of many disappointments for them in relation to their son and his new wife. Mum and Dad married just after New Year in 1970, going off to the local town hall in secret and announcing what they'd done after the fact. Molly and Harry were distraught that their son had wed without them there, but they were even more upset when they found out that their new daughter-in-law already had a child and was pregnant again – to another man.

Jennifer was born later that year. By that time everyone around them, family and friends, had agreed that Norman was one of the good guys. After all, a woman who had two children to a married man wasn't much of a catch. Mum's parents may have been unwittingly supporting her lifestyle by looking after Ian, but her name was still mud in the area where they all lived. Babies born out of wedlock were bastards back then, the women sluts or 'fallen women' and the men . . . well, the men tended to get away with it. It would have been perceived that, in marrying Norman Yeo, Mum had landed on her feet rather than her back for once. When he adopted Ian, and then Jennifer soon after she was born, it only added to the high esteem in which he was held.

As I grew up, I was used to hearing this from the people who knew our family. 'That man's a saint,' locals would say, when they became aware of what he'd done. Mum was the sinner, and he was the perfect saviour who had swooped in to save her and her bastards from a terrible life.

To the rest of the world, he was a good man, a great father, a loving husband – but the rest of the world can be very blind to a lot of things that go on behind closed doors. There was so much they didn't see. From an early stage, there was a problem in that Mum and Dad were just too much alike. They were both lazy, to the point of being bone idle, and their priorities were completely wrong. They acted as if they thought the world owed them a living, and they would never do anything for themselves if there was some poor mug who could be persuaded to do it for them.

My maternal nanny was never slow in telling me what she thought of the situation. She had taken care of Ian when he was born, and regretted it deeply. 'I was only trying to help out,' Ivy once said to me, 'but I made things a hundred times worse. I should have left her to it – if she'd had to do the hard work, who knows what might have happened? Maybe she wouldn't have been so quick to rush into having another one. I knew that your mother wouldn't scratch her own backside if she could find someone else to do it for her, and I should have realised that at the time.'

And now, with Norman, she'd found someone just as lazy and entitled as her.

It was a sad truth that things got a lot worse when she met Dad. They were two people who should never have got together. Rather than a saint and a sinner, they were as bad as each other, always looking at how they could make their own lives easier, and completely careless about who might get hurt in the process. Mum was a troublemaker, manipulative beyond belief; she also had the best memory of anyone I've ever met. She could recall any perceived slight, any dirty look, anyone who she decided had ever been a 'bitch' to her. Her own faults were nothing; she was a born bully but she always thought she was the victim. She certainly changed some aspects of Norman as soon as they wed, but a lot of that was down to how lazy he was anyway. He always went for the easy route, so when Mum wanted to spend lots of money on clothes for herself he didn't complain, he just saw it as a way of keeping her quiet. He only had one set of things to wear and couldn't have cared less if he smelled or was a state every day. Mum waltzed around in furs, while he wore the same outfit until it fell off him. She did seem to be the one calling the shots – which added to other people thinking he was a 'saint' – but I know that his idleness was behind a lot of it. He didn't need to be clean or dress well, as he never intended to work. He didn't need money, as Mum would always go running to her parents if she'd spent everything on herself and the kids needed feeding. They seemed to have no sense of responsibility whatsoever.

The newly-weds were given a flat in a popular area of the Wirral, which they duly complained about. Mum went to the council every day to shout about needing somewhere with a garden, somewhere bigger for the four of them. She could find a bit of energy when she thought she could get something for free, but the energy would never stretch to something as upstanding as employment.

Within a few months, they were moved to a ground-floor council maisonette, where they fought every day and drank every night and all weekend. They did nothing homely to that place; in fact, social work files from that period say that it was 'substandard' – a description of what the pair of them had done to it, not the state when they moved in.

Mum was a violent woman from the start, and she took a lot of it out on Norman, but she saved most of her hatred for my half-sister, Jennifer, and that's well documented in official files. Ian had spent a lot of time with Mum's parents since he was born, and it stayed that way when she married my father. However, Ivy and Bert hadn't developed that same link with Jenny. When Ian was still a baby, Mum was chasing after her married man, meeting up with him whenever she could, but by the time Jenny was born, she herself was married – it was far from perfect but she had a house and a husband, so Nanny and Granddad stepped back. They still looked after Ian a lot, though.

Mum got pregnant with me quite quickly, and I was born in 1971. She was always keen to show me the card Dad sent her, which said, 'Thank you for our beautiful baby', but the truth was, he ignored us for years. He was often away fishing, his excuse to escape from Mum, I think, and when he came back she would be waiting at the door to tell him what little shits we'd been and what a terrible time she'd had since he'd been gone. He could be violent at times, but she was the one who was constantly smashing windows and throwing things. She would try to scald us and hit us with the pots a lot of the time. She punched the front door in once in a fit of temper, and I remember from when I was very little that she set fire to the bed when Dad was in it. Another time she threw boiling water at him. There was no damage done to him, but it showed what she was capable of. I don't really remember much of my very early years apart from that constant backdrop of violence, but to me, it was normal. It was just how my family was; I didn't know any other way to live.

Mum was certainly more of a presence in my life to begin with, not just because Dad was away on his fishing trips so much but because she was loud and she was attention-seeking. She was always well-dressed and she always found the money to buy clothes and go to the hairdresser, even if it meant that her kids went short. It was the early 1970s and she liked to follow fashion. She wore minidresses and always had her make-up done, with brown lipstick and lots of black eyeliner. Her hair was dyed very dark, and she often had a perm – she always had a fad to follow. Dad was quite handsome, dark and tall, but he never cared about taking care of himself the way Mum did; he was far too lazy. I think I look like her – I don't see him in me at all, but perhaps that's just wishful thinking. I suppose there's a chance that he isn't even my dad, given how much Mum apparently slept around, but he claims he is, and I have to live with that.

The only good advice my dad ever gave me was never to have an argument with Mum. 'You'll never win,' he said, and he was absolutely right. From her, there was only ever one piece of advice: 'Go out with a man until a better one comes along.' That was, presumably, what she had always done, but I hate to think what the rest must have been like if Norman Yeo ended up looking like a good opportunity. I guess she must have gone for what other people saw – I'm not saying she fell for it, but she maybe wanted the superficiality of it looking like she had a 'respectable' family life, at least while it suited her.

There were two boys born after me. Both of them had Dad's characteristics and they were certainly treated better than me, Ian or Jenny. Andrew looked like my Grandma Molly, and Kevin looked like Granddad Harry – maybe that's why he took to them more. Maybe Mum liked them because they were boys, and they weren't from a man who she thought had deserted her when she had done all she could to get him.

She certainly treated them very differently from how she treated Jenny. She hated my sister from the day she was born, according to everyone who has told me stories over the years. Nanny Ivy always said that Jenny was just a quiet child, who would sit in the corner on her own, but I know why – she was trying to avoid her own mother. The mother who would tell people that Jenny pretended she couldn't walk, even though it was a barefaced lie. It was yet another way of making Jenny feel backward from an early age. She would also rub her soiled nappy in her face, something I remember so clearly and which was such a heartless thing to do to any child.

I remember seeing Mum do those things to Jenny from when I was tiny and I thought it was horrible. Why would a mummy behave like that? Why would a mummy be so mean to her little girl?

It seemed to just come naturally to her. The way she was coloured my life, coloured Jenny's life and made my childhood one of horror. It wasn't just her alone who did that but, my God, she laid the foundations, she truly did.

This is the story I have managed to pull together, Jenny, from the scraps of memories, the comments from family, the huge number of folders and files that I told you were scattered around me. It's the jigsaw of our lives, and I've barely got the corners in place, the edges sorted.

It's a strange thing to do, because I feel that I have to get this right, I have to give you a voice as much as I have to give me a voice, and I'll only get this one chance. I remember things that were said about our family, insults that were thrown at us, constant complaints from neighbours, but no one really knew what was going on. Those two tiny little girls, neither of them truly wanted, deserve everything to be out in the open now. My memories have to be bigger than the ones I actually own – they have to include yours, the things you told me in later life, the things other people told me, the things that were written down. I'm trying to put it all in one place, but it's overwhelming, Jenny. Every time I open those files, or open the memory box in my head, I feel as if the stories are desperate to be told, they're screaming at me. They have been kept locked up for so long, and now . . . now, they have a chance to be heard. Now we have a chance to be heard. It's an enormous responsibility, but I owe it to you, I owe it to us.

I only hope that other people can see the picture I'm trying to paint, because I need this story to give you a voice – and, by doing that, I want to give hope to all the other little girls and boys out there who never had a chance to tell their story either. We all deserve the opportunity to be heard, to write our own lines. When others do that for us, when they label us, it can chip away at our self-esteem so effectively that we end up blaming ourselves for the bad things – when we are told it is our fault, when we are told we brought it on ourselves, eventually we start to wonder if it's the truth. Maybe we did. Maybe we are weak or pathetic. In my dark moments, I have wondered about all of that, but I know it's just part of the psychological control I was subjected to. If I start to think – if *any* survivor starts to think – that they were responsible for their own abuse, the perpetrator has won. I won't let that happen. I'll remember, and I'll shout from the rooftops – we matter, all of us survivors matter. These are the things we have to remember – we need to tell ourselves, *you are good enough. You matter. You are special and you can overcome what was done to you.* But there is so much to overcome, Jenny, so very much.

CHAPTER 2

FOUNDATIONS
1970–1974

As a little girl, I believed everything Mum said to me. When you're small, you do – you do think that your mummy is telling the truth, that every word that comes from her mouth can't be challenged. Now though, when I look back, I can see that my childhood was littered with lies.

'Your granddad's a proper bastard,' she told me one time. 'He battered a pregnancy out of me once.'

It was a lie. She would often admit later that she had made things up once she'd seen the impact they'd had. I'd sit there, wide-eyed, far too young to really understand, and just react to the few words I could comprehend, trying to make sense of the other ones that were new and hard for me.

'I raised your nanny's bloody kids for her,' she'd sneer. 'I brought up my own brothers and sister from when I was six years old, and all that cow ever does is tell everyone that I'm a waste of space.'

Another lie. Another lie that was blown apart by her own siblings, who used to tell me how awful Mum had been as a child, and how they always tiptoed around her, wondering what she would do next. She constantly accused men of all being 'after her', and if they couldn't get her, she would say they'd raped her. She accused her own father-in-law of this, all the other men in our family, Jenny and Ian's dad, almost every man she met, and it was a pattern of behaviour she kept going for decades.

The lies kept on coming but I believed them all for years. Even when I started to question the things she had told me, I couldn't work out why she would have said them in the first place. Someone said to me recently that, to this day, she can't stop lying. She's rewritten her own past as one full of cruelty and misery, with hateful parents who never lifted a finger to help and a childhood in which she was expected to run around after everyone else; a good girl who was exploited by those who should have loved her. Lies, lies and more lies. My Auntie Jeanette once said to me, 'Your mum wakes up in the morning and all the stories she told the day before are the truth. It's as simple as that.' There are some people who tell lies even when the truth is easier – I sometimes wonder if that's what Mum does. It certainly often seemed that way.

My big sister Jennifer was born on 27 February 1970 in Wallasey. There are no happy stories of her birth, no staccato home movies or boxes of baby paraphernalia. It's not surprising really, given that she wasn't wanted. Mum, pregnant and unable to get the man she had set her sights on, was very open about how she felt from the start. Jennifer had been taken into care at eighteen months because she was bruised and undernourished, but I don't have all of those files as I wasn't yet born, so they are deemed 'not relevant' to me. However, later social work records show that not only was Mum open about not caring about her first daughter, she was violent towards her too. The foundations of her relationship with Jenny – and with me, as it would transpire – were not love and caring, but bitterness and cruelty.

On 16 August 1971 Mrs Yeo requested the reception into care of her children because of her pending admission into hospital for a minor operation. After this, no further contact was made for approximately one year when our current involvement began. On 10 August 1972, the Health Visitor discovered during a visit to the home that Jennifer was badly bruised – there was severe bruising on her forehead, arms, across her shoulder blades and extending down the lumbar-sacral region of her back. The department counselled with Mrs Yeo to allow her daughter to come into voluntary care. This was refused and a 28-day Place of Safety Order was taken.

Mrs Yeo states that she did not want Jennifer but she became pregnant to spite her parents. She married her husband very much against his mother's wishes. He is an only son. The marriage does not appear to be a harmonious one. The children are well clothed and well nourished. She states that when Jennifer is very naughty she slaps her around the eyes. (5 April 1972)

I find this entry strange for two reasons – we were most certainly *not* well-clothed and well-nourished, and there seems to be no criticism of Mum slapping a two-year-old. Jenny was only a toddler, barely more than a baby. Some people will say those were different times, but you would think that, when a family was already on the radar, any hint of violence would be picked up on. It seems that Mum didn't even bother trying to hide it, and I wonder why that is – did she feel she was untouchable, or was she admitting to 'slaps' rather than being open about the extent of what was happening? In fact, even Dad could see how bad things were as, at one point, he asked for Jenny to be taken into care as he 'feared his wife would kill her.'

Things certainly got worse, and, by August 1972, Jenny's poor little body was showing evidence of the terrible life she led.

Health visitor found Jennifer badly bruised – when examined, she was found to have sustained injury to cause severe bruising on the forehead, arms and across the shoulder blades extending to lumbar-sacral region of the back. She was weighed and found to be 12lbs 2oz in weight. After the doctor's visit that afternoon it was felt that Jennifer should be taken into care under Section 1 of the Children Act 1948. (10 August 1972)

Weighing only 12lbs at the age of almost two-and-a-half years; covered in bruises and injuries. This was too much even for those days, when children were often believed to need a good slap to keep them in line, and it was thought that they should be seen and not heard. The professionals who were involved tried to get Mum to admit Jenny into voluntary care and, quite openly, she told them that my sister had been a problem since the moment of conception. *'Throughout her pregnancy, Mrs Yeo did not want the child as the relationship between herself and the natural father was completely finished.'* Maybe this was just Mum being the person that Nanny had always said she was, thinking that she could do nothing wrong or believing that she could always get out of trouble, but it seems a very bald, uncaring statement to make to those who were involved in checking whether even more severe intervention was needed for our family.

Mum was unwilling to agree to anything until Dad got back later that day and, while they waited for him, the social workers decided that Jenny's injuries were consistent with a beating or several beatings very recently. When they went back to Mum at 4:30pm, she refused to let them take Jenny away, so a 'Place of Safety' action was deemed appropriate. Mum denied everything to do with Jenny's 'present state'. On that same day, there is a question in the file that asks, *'Do you consider any other members of the household at risk?'* The reply, in capital letters, is: *NO*. Whether that's wishful thinking or a complete ignorance of the facts, I have no idea – but it was a million miles from the truth.

The next month, a letter was sent by the police to the Senior Children's Officer of the Region. It makes for heartbreakingly stark reading – I do understand that the clinical way in which Jenny and her injuries are described is how these things have to be recorded, but I just want to reach out to that little girl and hold her tight.

*To the Senior Children's Officer of the Cheshire
Constabulary
    From the Chief Superintendent of the County
Borough of Wallasey*

Dear Sir –
*Complaint of assault on Jennifer Marie Yeo, 2
years.*
    *At 6pm on Thursday 10th August 1972,
a complaint was received at the Criminal
Investigation Department, Wallasey, from Mr
Surridge of your Department to the effect that the
above-named girl had been assaulted and the child
had been removed from the parental home and
placed in the care of the Local Authority under a
Place of Safety Order for 28 days.*
    *I have considered all the facts of this case which
was fully investigated [. . .] and have decided not
to take any further Police action in this matter.*
    Thanking you for your valuable assistance.
    Yours faithfully – Chief Superintendent
    13 September 1972

So, that was that – no further action taken. The police
might not have been interested, but the Yeo family file was
getting bigger every day. By this stage, there were three
of us kids (Ian, Jenny and me), and the social workers

were obviously keen to keep an eye on what was going on. A picture emerges of my mother and father in which much more attention is paid to her than to him. While that does reflect some of our family dynamic – Dad was always fishing, and too lazy to do much, while Mum was at home pretty much constantly – I think it also indicates the bias that made them feel that the home environment was very much the woman's domain. Anything Dad did around the home or with us was seen as 'helping' Mum, and the fact that they concentrated on her meant that he could get away with staying pretty inconspicuous.

Mr Yeo was not very communicative during our brief visit, he kept his head buried in the newspaper, which was scattered over the dining room table. His wife, who appears to be a boisterous personality, informed us that the children were keeping well. (23 January 1973)

The children looked fit and well. Mr Yeo is unemployed and he appears to give his wife a good deal of support in the home. Mr and Mrs Yeo are still suspicious of the Department because of what happened to Jennifer who was taken into care on a Place of Safety order. I feel it may be some time before I am accepted and they see me in a helpful capacity. Mr Yeo and his wife stated that they are subjected to a degree of hostility by their neighbours

because of the incident concerning Jennifer.
(25 January 1973)

Mr Yeo is still unemployed. He finds that from
a financial point of view he is better off on state
benefits than if he were in regular employment.
During the interview, one had the impression that
there is still a degree of rejection of Jennifer by her
mother . . . she stated that she had perhaps been a
little heavy-handed with the children, particularly
Jennifer, on past occasions, but [. . .] she now
counts to ten before she decides to discipline
the children. In this family, it would seem that
Mrs Yeo has a rather boisterous personality as a
dominant partner but as the interview progresses
it would seem that Mr Yeo, who has not been very
communicative on past interviews, may be the
dominant partner in the marriage and it is he who
may hold the unit together. (1 February 1973)

As I was only around two years old, I have no memory
of any of this and it's as if I'm seeing a picture painted of
our family by outside observers. I want to scream at them,
'Take Jenny away again – save her!', but there is also a
part of me that feels like I'm watching a film that doesn't
feature me, and I hope against hope that the mummy will
turn out to be a nicer person, that the daddy will make
it all better. I wonder if the social workers felt like that

too? Did they hope that one day they would turn up and everything would be fine? That Mum would open the door and exclaim, 'It's fine – I love them all!' Dad would be striding out, in a suit, off to work, the perfect little family playing happily in the background. Life doesn't work that way though, does it? Even the authorities could see that Dad was bone idle, and that Mum wanted all of the attention on her. The way in which she is described as 'boisterous' hides so much and I wish that the people writing these reports would just come out and say what they really mean.

As the interview progressed, Mrs Yeo clearly rejected Jennifer but her husband appears to take a more positive interest so he more or less compensates for her mother's lack of interest. . . . one would probably describe Mrs Yeo's relationship with her daughter as one of love and hate . . . If visitors or social workers are too attentive towards Jennifer, Mrs Yeo becomes easily upset, she becomes irritable. Mr Yeo is a butcher by trade . . . he agrees that to some extent he is basically a lazy man – his only interest appears to be in fishing. (22 February 1973)

Mr Yeo was on a fishing trip and Mrs Yeo opened up a bit. She told me that she hadn't been talking to her husband. In life, she has rushed from one male relationship to another. She stated that her husband was very sexually demanding of her – I suggested she should discuss this rather delicate area with her husband. (19 March 1973)

This 'delicate area' was one that would colour much of what went on in our childhood. I would find out in later years that my parents had a sex life that involved lots of other people, but there would be no way of the social workers discovering this. I think the records probably show things that they saw frequently rather than one-offs, as there is a lot of repetition; so, Dad's fishing trips no doubt infuriated them as they were his way of getting out of the house and avoiding gainful employment, and Mum's complaints about being 'hard done by' all her life seem to have registered too. They also noted, on many occasions, the way in which Mum was always irritated if Jenny's behaviour took the attention from her. Even when she was only three years old, it was as if a competition had been set up between the two of them, and Mum appeared desperate to win.

Jennifer was very attention seeking; right through the interview she continually played around my feet, brought many of her toys to me to see, climbed up on my knee. On several occasions, Mrs Yeo reprimanded her verbally for annoying me. It was

29

interesting to see that as soon as anyone displays any affection for Jennifer, Mrs Yeo gets very upset about this. (29 March 1973)

To me, that seems like such a twisted way to process your relationship with your own child. To have a rivalry with your toddler, to want the social worker to pay attention to you all the time and ignore the neglected, love-starved little one bringing them toys – it's pitiful. It's only natural for a small child to want attention, especially if they were being denied anything positive in their day-to-day life, and my heart breaks at the thought of young Jenny seeing new people coming in, hoping they would play with her or give her a cuddle, then watching as Mum tried to get all of the focus back on her.

The social workers did notice some things: '*I noticed that Jennifer had a bruise on her forehead and Mrs Yeo and her husband stated that she banged her head on the window.*' I want to, again, scream at them to do something, not just to make a note of it – they could already see some of what was happening, they already knew there was a battle between a grown-up and a little girl, they already had Mum's admissions that she hit Jenny, so why were bruises ignored and excuses accepted?

Every so often, there is a phrase in the files that makes me wonder if things are changing, if this is it – is this where the cavalry arrives? One such comment, written in

May 1973, stabs at my heart: *how terribly difficult it is for these children to come to terms with the vagaries of their parents' whims.* It goes on: *there is rejection of Jennifer by her mother and she is possibly 'heavy-handed' when she disciplines the children, but there is nothing substantial if one wanted to remove Jennifer.* The vagaries of parents, and heavy-handed mothering, were by no means enough to rescue Jenny, and when my time came they would not be enough to rescue me either.

I am torn between recognising that the social workers were keeping an eye on us and acknowledging that there was something to be wary of, and seeing that they were not actually doing much about it. Jenny's injuries were getting more frequent and more severe, but I wonder how many they never even knew of, given that it would only be the ones they could see, or the ones that required medical treatment, which registered. Only a month after the somewhat veiled reference to Mum being 'heavy-handed' came one such official presentation, when Jenny had to be taken to hospital.

Mrs Yeo informed me that Jennifer had another bad fall and she had taken her to the hospital – while there, Jennifer told the doctor that a relation had pushed her down the stairs. Mrs Yeo gave her a smacking for this. There is a strong possibility that Jennifer may be severely physically disciplined by

her mother who states that she has 'very little time'
for Jennifer. Too often, this little girl has bruises on
her face and her mother states that she has had a
fall. Jennifer appears to be rejected by her mother.
(29 June 1973)

The reports constantly state that Mum doesn't want
Jenny to go to playgroup, that she distrusts people, that
she doesn't want to be 'watched'. They know she rejected
my sister, as they note it down time and time again, but at
times they do withdraw – presumably they had to do this
if my parents requested it, as no complaint was actually
being pressed at that time. Who, indeed, could have
complained? Us little children, with no voice, no ability to
do so? The only hope we had was that we would be hit so
hard that it would go further – what a thing to wish for.

They have asked me not to visit again. They are
of the opinion that with my regular visiting, they
are being watched – the neighbours are inquisitive
about a welfare officer visiting. I explained to Mrs
Yeo that I would not call again but if she ever
wanted advice or help, she could contact me.
(3 August 1973)

While the social workers may have been forced to
retreat for a while, thankfully the 'inquisitive' neighbours

were still watching. By September 1973, one of them had made a telephone complaint to say that *'Jennifer had a badly bruised face.'* They asked that someone make a visit *'as soon as possible'*, and the department actually ensured that happened later that day, which makes me think they were waiting for a reason to resume contact. A social worker called Mr Curran was told by Mum that Jenny 'was always falling and banging herself'. This seems to have provided an opportunity for supervision to recommence and, the following week, some action was finally taken. A health visitor by the name of Miss Reynolds noticed that Jenny had

. . . severe facial bruising and asked Mrs Yeo to call the family doctor – she said that Jennifer had fallen off a wall. Social worker visited Dr Meldrum who was of the opinion that Jennifer's bruises could not have been caused by a fall. Possibility of 'battered baby'. Discussed case and decided to take a Place of Safety Order. Visited [. . .] where Mrs Yeo refused to let me see Jennifer and promised to bring Jennifer to the Department. Arranged court for 4:30pm. Mr Yeo visited and the position was explained fully. At 4:15pm, social worker went to their home and Mrs Yeo and Jennifer were leaving. I escorted them to Court where an application for a PSO was granted fully. (17 September 1973)

I breathed a sigh of relief when I read that – even though it had already happened, in real life, years ago.

> That was it, Jenny – you were out. I know you had been taken away once before, but this time seemed different. There were so many people watching, so many people waiting for one of our parents to make a wrong move, or to let them see something they had hidden so well for so long – and, now they had. The Place of Safety Order was applied for. I wish that I could feel some hope, I wish I could feel that this was the start of it getting better, but I know the next few chapters of your story all too well. They are seeing some of it, but they don't see it all, and they don't give you what you need. The 'vagaries' are still there; the little girl is still lost.

Jenny was placed temporarily with a woman called Mrs Fenlon, and arrangements were made for an examination the next day. The results of that examination resulted in Jenny being sent to Birkenhead Children's Hospital. The files state:

> *I am of the opinion that Mrs Yeo still rejects Jennifer . . . on previous visits, I have discussed this mother/child relationship, but Mrs Yeo acts*

like another child when Jennifer is difficult. I have discussed with her the discipline of the children, particularly Jennifer, and she states that when she is very naughty, she slaps her. (19 September 1973)

The files are bulky at this point and, as I read them, I'm getting dizzy. There's so much to take in, and I feel as if I'm whirling around between the past that I'm reading about, the past that I experienced and the future I know is coming – it's a story where I already know the ending, and there are so many voices shouting at me at once. Putting Jenny on the 'At Risk' register due to the bruising that was visible was the first step towards getting some sort of more established involvement for her, and letters were being sent thick and fast between all agencies and departments. In the middle of it is a comment made by Jenny's foster-mother, Mrs Fenlon, which says so much.

'*[She] describes Jennifer as a happy, talkative, responsive child, with a healthy appetite. Jennifer appears a little frightened of adults.*' Already the foster-family could see how lovely Jenny could be when she felt safe, but they could also tell there was something that had brought about this reticence with adults. It was unsurprising given what I knew and given what I found in the files – a letter from the Birkenhead Children's Hospital that bluntly laid out just what Jenny had endured.

Jennifer was admitted from Casualty on 18 September 1973. No history was available as the child was brought in by a social worker. On examination, the child was fully conscious. The following injuries were found on her body:

Head – haematoma in her left parietal region 3" x 4", and in the right parietal region 1"x 1".

Eyes – both eyes were bruised around the lids, right more than left.

Bruises over the left clavicle, and ecchymoses over both arms, and over both forearms.

Shoulders – bruises over the left shoulder.

Left buttock – large bruise.

Right buttock – healing lesion, probably a superficial burn.

Shins – multiple small bruises over both shins.

Left foot – healed linear scar over dorsum of left foot.

Signed Dr Shahbazi, 3 October 1973

It was a hideous shopping list of abuse and it led to a care order being imposed on 8 October 1973, under the reason of *'her proper development being avoidably impaired or neglected'*. When I read that list, when I see the clear medical awareness of what was done to my sister, I can't help but shake. I'm in my own home, reading it all, remembering it all, but at the centre of everything is a tiny little body all those years ago, with violence and hatred being rained down on it every single day. That the only escape was to be beaten so much that something could finally be done to take Jenny away is unbearably cruel and, as always, I can't fathom how a mother and father could do all of that to their child, or how anyone could do that to any child. The following week, Jenny was taken in by a foster-carer called Mrs Cain, who reported her to be a bit of a handful to start with, before she 'starts to conform'. What I see from that is an acting-out child who has only known awful things, and who now sees that she needs to behave in a certain way.

She looks very happy and chatters incessantly – they call her Yo-yo because she will not sit still. She has on two occasions asked Mrs Cain not to let her go home to her horrible mummy who always hits her. She does not speak of her father. She often asks for verbal affirmation that she is loved. Mrs Cain enquired whether Jennifer would definitely be in the care of the local authority until she is 18. I told her that Mrs Yeo can go back to Court at any time and that the decision must rest with the Court. She was obviously anxious that J should not be taken from them in a few years' time.

By November, for unspecified reasons, Mum had been offered psychiatric treatment – which she refused. A letter from a consultant to the various workers involved with our family tried to summarise the situation so far, in just one page, but it makes for dire reading. Not only is it full of Mum's lies, which they often accepted and repeated, but it shows many missed opportunities:

Thank you for asking me to see Mrs Yeo at her home yesterday [. . .]Jennifer, aged 3 and a half, was taken into care some two months ago as a battered baby, and Mrs Yeo was told the child would remain there until she was 18. This girl was brought up in a very violent and unhappy home

'This girl' was my mother. Yet there was absolutely no evidence of her home being violent or unhappy.

The following month (December 1973), the Cains asked for Jenny to be taken away from them. A photocopy of a letter handwritten in loopy script in the files from Mrs Cain says:

This is a rather difficult letter to write, but I think I can get my feelings down on paper, rather than try to explain over the phone.

I have in my care at the moment Jennifer Yeo, and would like to ask you if you could possibly find her a new home. This is partly because she is quite a difficult child to handle with three others, but mainly because although I thought I could accept another child into the family, I find I can't. I can't really explain why to you.

I know you will be disappointed for Jennifer's sake, and I feel very sorry for the poor little one, she has had so much ill-treatment in the past. She is progressing very well physically, putting on weight, rosy cheeks etc.

I would also like to say that you don't have to rush around to find her another home as we are not in any desperate hurry for her to go.

Yours faithfully – Glenda Cain.

Then KEEP HER! I want to shout. KEEP MY SISTER! Give her a chance, please give her a chance. If you're in no desperate hurry for her to go, please don't send her to someone else – give her a chance and you'll love her, I swear you'll love her.

Mrs Cain seemed to have second thoughts for a while. When the social worker visited after the letter was received, the following report was filed:

Her opening remark was: 'I do not know why I wrote now. I was at my wits' end and the situation has improved'. *She has found that the relationship between herself and Jennifer has been a constant battle and she felt she could not cope. Eventually her husband had a long chat with Jennifer and since then the situation has improved. The behaviour exhibited includes pouring Vim, soap powder, etc., over the floor many times daily, marking walls, etc., a general coarseness of speech which the Cains are not used to. She also tries to play one off against the other.*

Jennifer often asks, 'Do you like me?' and 'Will you cry if I leave you?' The latter especially when she has been in trouble and has decided to return to 'Auntie Cissy' (Mrs Fenton – previous foster-parent). She also shows fear of not being fed at mealtimes. The three boys have all accepted Yo-yo quite readily and the middle child plays with her a great deal. The only sign of jealousy has come from the youngest boy. Yo-yo is a happy, noisy, naughty child, who remains over-affectionate. There is perhaps a lack of 'cuddly love' in the foster home at present. The Enuresis continues and a special allowance has been applied for.

I discussed with Mrs Cain the emotional involvement and the differences between her feeling towards her own children and towards Yo-yo. She needs security and if there is any rejection by the foster-parents, this may reinforce the pattern set up by her parents. Mrs Cain thinks she will be able to assess whether she can cope with Yo-yo in about two weeks' time; I suggested that the situation would fluctuate and difficulties may continue to occur.

This was one of the saddest things I had read so far. The extent of Jenny's behavioural problems, the detail of it, was something I had been unaware of until now. In my mind's eye, I could see the little girl who was so lost, so confused, swearing, pouring soap powder all over, trying to manipulate strangers into loving her, and it was heartbreaking. Ultimately, Mrs Cain decided she couldn't go on with it, and Jenny's options were to go back to Mrs Fenlon or return to a care home again on a short-term placement. Mrs Fenlon agreed to take her back, *'where she had made a good relationship and was very much wanted'*, and I am so glad they did that for her at that time. Jenny must have been glad too, as the files say: *'She was very excited about the move and within five minutes of arrival had made herself completely at home.'* Within a few weeks, it's noted that she's no longer soiling her clothes and there is a *'resultant diminishing of her behavioural problems'*.

I really do feel that Jenny needed stability and a non-threatening environment, but the overriding problem was that Mum kept changing her mind; she would say that she didn't want Jenny back, then she did. She would lay down rules and regulations one minute, trying to control everything, then, the next, say that she never wanted to be reconciled with my sister anyway.

At the start of 1974, there are some of the first comments about me. I am '*the little girl*' who Mum claims has '*signs*' of '*beginning to react as Jennifer has, i.e, she says that she has Jennifer's dirty habits.*' There are also comments about police visits at this stage, but no details, and I have few memories of that stage of my life. I can only assume that I was wetting the bed, or that Mum was claiming that to be the case, and that I was doing so for the same reasons as Jenny.

There is so much between the lines of what is written in the files, and I feel there are often comments recorded there that are not expanded upon, but left for interpretation. Maybe the social workers could only say so much, maybe their hands were tied, but sometimes I can't help but pick up on what is playing out in front of me, even when it's written in very few words. '*Jenny met Mum in an interview room and asks if she can come home – Mum says only when she is 'better'* . . . '*Mrs Yeo was most concerned that Jennifer call her Lesley and Mr Yeo Norman. Jenny showed no emotion when she left her mother. (21 January 1974)*'

***

The only hope for some security and stability in Jenny's life was the foster-mother, Mrs Fenlon, but even this wasn't progressing well. Although it seemed as if the woman had worked wonders with Jenny's bed-wetting, and had been loving towards her, in January 1974 it was noted that she didn't want to continue as a long-term foster-parent as she felt that she was:

> . . . *too old to undertake such a role. However, her daughter would very much like to foster Jennifer. This will be investigated. Jennifer is a difficult child. She has a good relationship with Mrs Fenlon's daughter and it may be advisable to transfer her to foster-parents she already knows.*

I wonder if my parents were told about this potential change, because at the next visit, it's clear to the social worker that something is wrong with *me* – in retrospect, perhaps the frustration about the situation with Jenny had resulted in the first obvious physical marks on me.

> *Karen Yeo has a cut on her face. I did not see Karen during the visit but Mrs Yeo informed me that the dog had pushed Karen over. It seemed quite reasonable to accept this. However, a close watch will have to be kept on the situation. The dog has now been taken away and they have a new puppy.*
> *(31 January 1974)*

This is a hurtful memory for me, and not because of the cut face. Animals, especially dogs, were used to as a method of taunting us for years. No sooner would I get attached to a new puppy than I would be told it would have to go as it didn't fit in, or was naughty, or Mum had too much to do. Dad could be horribly cruel with them, often throwing them out into the street or hitting them. To this day, I adore animals, and my own dogs have always been like my babies to me. I know this comes from all of the puppies that were taken from me when I was growing up; and the casual way in which the files say that one dog was taken away and replaced by a new puppy, as if they were all interchangeable, cuts deeper than you could imagine.

Do you remember any of the animals, Jenny? They changed so often for me, so I imagine it would be even more confusing for you. Perhaps you never let yourself get attached – you would never know if they would be there from one visit to the next – but it was the same for me, except it was on an hour-by-hour basis. I could leave a dog in the living room while I toddled off somewhere else, and by the time I went back, Mum would be screaming that she couldn't deal with it any more and Dad would be dragging it away, never to be seen again. I did cry, I know I did, and I never managed to harden myself to it. Every new puppy was another little life to fall in love with. I still do it; I still fall head over heels every time an animal comes into my life, and I'm glad of that. I'm glad they didn't break that feeling I have that every soul matters.

It's funny the stuff that gets you after all these years, Jenny. I'm crying for you as I read these files – even though I'm probably trying to distance myself by focusing on the facts of it all – but I'm crying for all those dogs too, the ones who ended up God knows where, thrown out into the streets, given to horrible people. I believe that you can tell a lot about someone by how they treat animals. Animals and children, that's how you know. And we knew, didn't we, Jenny? We knew.

At the end of January 1974, there was an attempt made to summarise our family history up until that point. There is, as always, so much hidden in what is not said, and the authorities even have to leave out some of what they have previously included, as there is so much to contend with. In two pages of faded type, they go over it all again, and also – again – include many of the pieces of the story they have been told and which, I suppose, they have to accept:

Mr and Mrs Yeo married on 14.1.70. Mr Yeo adopted the two eldest children about September 1970. Mrs

45

Yeo states that if any distinction has been made by him between the four children, Jennifer has been the favourite. Mrs Yeo has said that although both Ian and Jennifer are not Mr Yeo's children, it has been Jennifer who has caused difficulty, almost from the moment of conception. Throughout her pregnancy, Mrs Yeo did not want the child. However, when she gave birth to Jennifer, she felt that she wanted to keep her despite the hardships the decision might involve. From her birth, Jennifer was apparently a difficult and uncooperative baby, who cried persistently, despite Mrs Yeo's efforts to comfort her. Mrs Yeo was convinced this behaviour occurred because Jennifer sensed her mother's initial rejection.

On 5.8.71 Mr Yeo was seen in the Duty Room of the Social Services Department where he explained why he had taken Jennifer away from Mrs Yeo and gone to live with his mother. He alleged that his wife had ill-treated Jennifer and had always taken it out on her, because she reminded her of the father. She had allegedly beaten her several times, the last time being the previous weekend. The child was examined the same day and the doctor reported bruises on both cheeks, buttocks, and the lumbar region and also both legs.

On 8.8.71, Mrs Yeo requested that all three children should be taken into care as she was going into hospital for an operation and Mr Yeo could not care for them. Mr Yeo was, by the time, back at home. On 16.8.71, the children were received into care.

On 16.8.71, Mr Yeo was visited and staff expressed concern about the child returning to the care of her mother. Mr Yeo admitted his wife had always been against the child but he was on the defensive and not prepared to discuss her attitudes in any detail. It was clear that he could not be relied upon to support his first story and so it seemed probable that the only possible action would be with the parents' consent.

Mr Yeo agreed to discuss with his wife the possibility of Jennifer remaining in care for a further period.

On 20.8.71, due to the hospitalisation of the foster-mother, Jennifer and Karen were transferred to separate foster-parents.

On 3.9.71, all three were discharged from the care of the Local Authority.

On 9.8.72, a referral was made, stating that the baby was in hospital, possibly with a fractured skull.

10.8.72, Jennifer was found to have bruising on her forehead, arms, across her shoulder blades and extending down to the lumbar-sacral region of her back. The social worker tried to gain the cooperation of Mrs Yeo, hoping to receive Jennifer into care on a voluntary basis. Eventually it was necessary to take a Place of Safety Order. At the end of the 28-day order, Jennifer remained in care under Section 1.

24.12.72 Jennifer returned home and the family was supervised by a social worker.

3.8.73 At the request of Mrs Yeo, and because the situation seemed a great deal more settled, supervision discontinued.

10.9.73 An anonymous caller informed the Department that Jennifer had a badly bruised face. A social worker visited the house and saw Jennifer. Mrs Yeo's explanation, that she was always falling and banging herself, was accepted.

17.9.73 A Place of Safety Order was taken on Jennifer, who had bad bruising of the face and body. Jennifer was placed with foster-parents.

18.9.73 Following an examination, Jennifer was admitted to hospital.

24.9.73 Jennifer was discharged from hospital to foster-parents.

18.10.73 Jennifer was transferred to long-term foster-parents.

3.12.73 Due to a breakdown in the fostering arrangements, Jennifer was replaced with short-term foster-parents.

January 1974 The Police interviewed Mr and Mrs Yeo about the incident.

*21.1.74 Mrs Yeo saw Jennifer and Jennifer asked
if she could go live with her mother.*

While that report ends, another has as its recommendation at the same time: '*I am of the opinion that Jennifer has been 'scapegoated' in her family; her relationship with her parent/parents was lacking the emotional harmony essential for her overall development and to prevent her from being maladjusted. I would, therefore, recommend that Jennifer be committed to the Care of the Local Authority on a Care Order.*'

All of this. All of these opportunities missed. Jenny passed from pillar to post, all four of us in and out of care, foster-families changing their minds, social workers either falling for lies or not being able to make the change that was needed – so many chances to change the ending of the story.

CHAPTER 3

A BROKEN,
TWISTED WORLD
1974–1977

Jenny was visiting us quite regularly at this time. The social workers were keeping an eye on the whole family situation, but they were also hoping that she could be returned to us. From what I read, they were wishing for a fairytale ending as much as I was. Also, from what I have discovered reading round this issue in later years, the idea of 'restoration', or making sure families were united again even if a child or children had been taken into care, was a very popular one. So, Jenny would sometimes be at home, or sometimes not – but, when she was back with us, my parents didn't even try to hide some of the appalling ways they treated her.

*Jenny was still in bed at 11:15am when the health
visitor arrived. Jenny was restrained in the bed with
her outspread hands and arms tied down. The child
had had nothing to eat since midday the previous
day. Her body was marked at that stage. Jenny was
ravenously hungry. (The HV took her to nursery
and informed the Social Services Department).*
(11 February 1974)

While a new potential foster-parent was found – a Mrs
Powell, who was *'very willing . . . it is hoped that Jennifer
will be moved there towards the end of the month'* –
*'Concern was expressed that Mrs Yeo was verbalising
her feelings that Karen is beginning to behave as Jennifer
behaved. It was therefore decided that a careful watch
should be kept on the situation.'* This was in March 1974,
while Mum was seeing Jenny every month. Dad was
usually fishing and I really don't think he had much of a
relationship with her at all. When Jenny did come back,
she was treated so cruelly. I knew that she would turn up
at the door with her little bag, packed with the few things
she owned, and Mum would say, 'Piss off – no one wants
you here,' and slam the door in her face. I don't know
what happened. I think she just sat and cried there until
Mum changed her mind, but I do know she did that quite
a few times – when Jenny got older, Mum often didn't let
her in, telling her that her siblings hated her and she was

to leave, and she always called her 'the pig'. It was Jenny herself who told me this when we were older and we used to reflect back on our lives, how we were separated so often but also going through so much that was similar.

Thankfully, the placement with Mrs Powell went ahead.

I was amazed at the difference in her. She has put on quite a lot of weight and seemed very relaxed. During her first two days with Mrs Powell, Jenny was very suspicious and nervous. Since then, she has become gradually more relaxed. She is obviously very much loved by the whole family. The GP thinks Jenny might be deaf in one ear.
(2 April 1974)

Jenny was indeed deaf in one ear, and it would be noted in later reports that this was from the physical abuse she had suffered when she was little more than a baby. She had been hit so hard that it affected her hearing for ever.

Mum was always shouting and always swearing. I can hardly think of a time she spoke to me without including some profanities – and my memories were starting to come through by this stage. For a child of three, four years of age to have that sort of nastiness being spewed at them constantly is awful, but it also becomes their normality. '*She was shouting at Karen when I arrived and was very offhand with her. Karen was very tense and eyed her mother continuously. Mrs Yeo threatened her several times. Mrs Yeo was verbally very aggressive. (3 April 1974)'* The notes state that bruises were noticed on me the next day, so I wonder if there were follow-up visits when things looked particularly bad. They weren't looking good for Jenny either, as the foster-family was starting to report problems.

J is causing tension between Mrs Powell and her daughter. She is with Mrs Powell all day and resents the rest of the family when they come home in the evening. Mrs Powell is very protective towards Jenny and takes her side against her daughter. Jenny realises this and uses it. Mrs Powell requests Jenny's removal. (9 May 1974)

The permanent return of Jenny to the family home (such as it was) seemed to be out of the question, perhaps because the social workers could see that Mum was doing the same to me, and telling them that I was turning out like my big sister, so a request was made to transfer her to a 'residential establishment'. The passing of Jenny from pillar to post had begun in earnest – and it would go on for the rest of her life. A heartbreaking letter from a consultant psychiatrist in June 1974 says that she was sent to him for 'disturbed emotions' and in that letter is a tear-jerking summary of everything that has already gone wrong in her life.

I examined the above-named child at this clinic this afternoon. Jennifer was four on 27th February. She belongs to that small unhappy band of children labelled by the sensational press 'the battered babies'. Twice in the first three years of her life she has had to be rescued from the vicious assaults of her mother. She was first taken into care briefly three years ago but returned to the care of her parents after a matter of months. She came into care again last September. Since then there have been three or four failed fosterings.

Jennifer is a bright, chatty, disinhibited little girl. So long as she is getting all of her own way she can be of sunny disposition. However, she is unable to tolerate frustration of any kind and quickly becomes fractious if any of her self-indulgent behaviour is checked.

She has a remarkably good use of language. She constantly importunes for attention. I am afraid it is unlikely that an ordinary fostering would be successful at this stage unless one were lucky enough to find a dedicated set of foster-parents endowed with unlimited patience.

Oh, Jenny – in that one letter you're being written off already, aren't you? You're the child from a media headline; you're a little girl whose only hope is to be 'lucky enough' to find foster-parents with unlimited patience. I wonder what you would have become if you had found those perfect foster-parents? I really do feel that many of those who tried were good people, but there were circumstances they couldn't control, or their own family demands got in the way of helping you. The awful thing is, you were one of so many – and so many children are *still* in exactly the same position. So much effort is put into keeping families together when the truth is, some homes are just toxic. Some people should never have children.

With a lack of suitable foster-parents, Jenny was moved into residential accommodation in a place called Newton Hall. By April 1975, it was being noted that she wasn't that bothered when our parents left if they ever did make the effort to see her in the first place – she thought of them as Norman and Lesley, and staff had to remind her of their relationship. Mum wasn't happy with this and I'm sure it led to her deciding that she didn't want her eldest daughter back at all – for the moment. *'This is the first time that Mrs Yeo has made any suggestion that she does not want Jennifer home. Mr Yeo's remarks were rather insignificant and insipid. I am beginning to wonder if they are really interested in Jennifer's future.'* (19 June 1975)

Looking at the files, it seems to me that something has obviously been very badly fractured; maybe, as Jenny was getting older, she had more of an awareness of how badly she had been treated, and of how she continued to be seen as just an awkward part of our parents' lives. By June that year, even the social worker was finally beginning to recognise the lies and manipulation and broken promises. Mum was saying that she didn't see any point in making the effort to visit Jenny if she would be in care until she was eighteen, or that she had no money – even though she was told she could apply for travelling expenses – or no one to look after us, and that we couldn't go as we got travel-sick. All lies. Letters constantly repeat that they showed 'no initiative' while she was at Newton Hall. Mum always made excuses about visiting her there, plans never came to anything and she would always suggest that Jenny came home, which was not something that was supported when she and Dad made no effort to see her elsewhere.

There was a new baby in our family by this point, which must have been so unsettling for Jenny. I can't help but think she must have wondered why Mum and Dad had another baby – and kept it at home – when she was unloved and unwanted, now in a residential home in Frodsham. In April 1976, Jenny visited to see baby Kevin and was left for an hour by the social worker. While she was away, my sister visited the bathroom, which obviously triggered memories of when Mum used to flush her head down the loo as punishment; there was an awful scene, which was still going on when the social worker returned. She rightly noted: '*I don't honestly know if these two could ever live together – I doubt it.*'

With Jenny at Frodsham, there should have been more of a settled sense to everything, but Mum was still up to her tricks of claiming that she wanted her back, then she didn't want her. She wanted to see her, then she didn't want to see her. Everything had to be on Mum's terms, and sometimes it's beyond belief to think that these power games were with a six-year-old child. While it didn't escape the eyes of the social work team, they could only express their frustration rather than put an end to it, given that parental rights were always to be considered.

Mrs Yeo was in a belligerent mood today – the worst I have seen her. She insists she wants Jennifer home and she will go to Court. She talked a lot of nonsense. I told her she could go to Frodsham at any time but, of course, this is always countered by the usual excuses. She told us Mr Yeo went out fishing in the mornings and was out looking for jobs in the afternoon – he obviously has his priorities the right way round! Except, of course, we are fairly certain he isn't looking for work any time of the day. I feel things are probably going to get difficult, but, if she wishes, she can apply to the Courts. We would oppose the application most strongly. I'm afraid Mrs Yeo only convinced us more than ever of her unsuitability of having Jennifer and her complete lack of understanding of the situation.

We saw the other children in the family and there does not appear to be any cause for concern. [. . .] Jennifer expressed disappointment that she was not going to see her mummy and daddy; she changes her mood and her mind by the minute.
(29 July 1976)

They may have been right about some things but, while they were starting in many ways to get a clear view of what my parents were like, in others they were wrong to think there was no cause for concern. My life was still one of shouting and emotional abuse. I was never shown any love, never cuddled, never made to think I was anything other than an inconvenience. Mum never spoke to me without calling me names, and my normality was one of coldness at best. She was doing to me what it seemed she had done to Jenny.

My first day at school was a happy time. It's not that anything was made of it before I started – there was no happy build-up or excitement as we chose my uniform and bag – but I did look forward to finally being a big girl, and escaping home every weekday. The classroom seemed huge after our crowded, messy house. There was a massive – or so it seemed – plastic Wendy house, with pots and pans, which was my favourite thing of all. I adored playing in there, making my own little world, and pretending that I was the mummy. The good mummy who

59

made lovely food for her kiddies and ensured everything was spotless. Despite the happiness there, though, there was always the worry in the back of my mind that I was doing something wrong. I hadn't really been socialised and my sense of normality was totally skewed.

We were all isolated from our neighbours and were never taken anywhere really; it was certainly a very rare occasion when we went to someone else's house. I had no friends. My world was my siblings, my family, anyone who came to our house to have sex with my parents – and social workers. And from that came worry. Once I was out in the world, I didn't really know what to do. I always thought I was stupid because that was all I had ever been told. I still think that way to this day, and suspect I always will. There was always a little voice inside my head that did me down. 'You're dilatory,' Mum would scream. 'Fucking dilatory.' That was her favourite word for me, and I must have heard it thousands of times over the years, even though I didn't really even know what it meant. One year, I even got a card from my brothers that said, 'Happy Birthday – we love you even though you are a bit slow.'

Sometimes I would cry and then get on with things – sometimes I still do that – but mostly I assumed that anything that went wrong was my fault. I felt there was a blackness inside me that other people could see; I could be chatty and friendly, but I felt that once people got to

60

know me, they'd see it. At school, I was quiet, I always sat at the back and I was no trouble; I never acted out. But, the truth was, I had no chance to ever be what I could have been. There was no one to do homework with me, no one to check it, no one to encourage me. I never had anyone say, 'Well done' as I learned my ABC, or take my hand as I went down steps, counting as we went. No one sang songs that taught me the colours of the rainbow, no one made animal noises as they pretended we were in a farmyard. There was no colour, no joy in my childhood. From as far back as I can remember, we all had chores. We cleaned for Mum – she would never lift a finger to do that – and it always took priority over schoolwork.

From the records, I can see that the social workers did sometimes come out of the blue rather than making an appointment, so they must have suspected more than they let on in the reports. I assume that they were trying to see our family as it really was, but on those occasions Mum just wouldn't let them in.

Even when my sister was removed from the situation, Mum's power was still strong. '*It is interesting to note – and I told Mrs Yeo – whenever she tells Jennifer she can come home if she stops wetting the bed, this in fact increases Jennifer's enuresis. (20 October 1976)*'

She was getting better at school by this point, and upset when she didn't do well in tests, which was progress as, previously, she hadn't cared. She was even Mary in the nativity play – although no one was there to see her. She was benefitting from the stability of residential care, but, from the records, everything seems very fragile.

Jenny's case was reviewed in the middle of February 1977, and five months later a letter was sent to a Mr Carpenter at the National Children's Home in Frodsham, from a Mr H.J. Surridge, who was the Area Social Services Officer. They noted that during the February review it had been decided that efforts would be made to 'find suitable contacts for Jennifer with a view to fostering in the long term.' A young couple in Wallasey were then contacted – Mr and Mrs Bill and Linda Jones – who were approved foster-parents. Linda is described in the letter as 'a very calm, sensible girl . . . an ex-nursery nurse', and the note coolly states that the couple 'are willing to participate in the experiment'. My sister – the experiment. Jenny was taken to meet them and they were 'anxious to commence the experiment' with a view to a week's trial during the summer holidays. Next step would be to get our mother to agree, which they expected would be difficult. Actually, she did agree.

By September 1977, Dad was making his dislike of the suggestions clear – records say that the social workers 'sense obstruction' and 'instances of non-cooperation'. The record then goes on to say that *'Mr Yeo eventually suggested we should not proceed with the foster-parent arrangement – although this had been their suggestion –*

and that we should arrange for Jennifer to have weekend visits home. The situation will be carefully monitored.'

Except it wasn't, was it? Jenny was staying at Newton Hall by this time, and there was some stability, but the fact that there were still attempts at restoration and she was still going back home, I feel, made things harder. It was one step forward, two steps back – any progress that was made, whether on bed-wetting or behaviour, was always negated once the horror of home was inflicted on her once again. Naturally, Mum managed to swing between one thing and another, acting happy and then changing her mind, saying getting Jenny back was all she wanted, only to then, when she needed attention, claim she couldn't deal with it. *'I later called to tell Mrs Yeo of the arrangement – she appeared delighted. Mrs Yeo stated to me that should she feel at any time that she cannot cope with Jennifer, she will tell me and we will revert to day visits.' (25 September 1977)*

At the start of October 1977 Jenny was picked up by her social worker, a Miss Williams, and brought to see us all in Abbotsford Street – Mum was warned not to say anything 'derisory' about Jenny's bed-wetting, as she was very sensitive about it. After the weekend at home, Williams noted that the bed-wetting *'wasn't too bad and Mrs Yeo had coped nobly!!'* She did seem to realise that this was unlikely to be the way things would be if Jenny stayed more often – *'I know this is a "honeymoon" and no way reflects the future, but it is a start. The children get on very well together and there were protestations all round when we left. Her first comment to the nun in charge was, "My mummy wants me to go home for Christmas."'*

This was downright manipulation in my eyes – how could a little girl fail to want to be home for Christmas? I know that, by this stage, I was being told that Jenny didn't want to stay with us, that she hated us and thought she was better than us. Mum tried to create barriers and to set us against each other, and, to a large extent, she succeeded. Jenny, as I later found out, was being told that we didn't want her, that we had a lovely time without her, and that we all would be happier if we never saw her again. Such cruelty. Such lies.

In the middle of this are two tiny little girls, Jenny. I read that you were '3ft 8 inches and 3st 4 and a half pounds' at this stage, and it breaks me. I have no idea what size I was, but there is a photo from then – one of the very few I have – and we are both just scraps. I just can't comprehend how anyone can inflict cruelty on children so small, on any child at all.

The thing is, I know what is coming, I know it's going to get even worse. My own memories are starting to come through, not just what I remember Mum saying about you, but the way everything was coming together – mental, emotional, physical cruelty. And both of us, kept apart and set against each other, when we could have been battling it together. I wonder what would have happened if we had been kept in the same house, all the time? Would we have been a little team, would we have given each other comfort? I know that's a pipedream, that I am inventing things, but I wish we had been given the chance, Jenny, I wish we could have fought it together. Maybe that would have changed the next chapters in our lives, who knows?

Jenny stayed at Frodsham for some time, and all I remember was that she continued to be in and out of our lives. I don't really have memories of what she liked or disliked, and when I read of these things in the files, they open up to me as a surprise – the elements of a sister I wasn't really allowed to know.

Her main interests are dolls, books, and attending Brownies. Rehabilitation is a possibility in the long-term future and we must now work towards this, forgetting about the idea of fostering. There have been no letters from parents. Jennifer moved to Junior 1 in September 1977, and has settled into

the class reasonably well. She is very full of her own
importance and takes a poor view of having to wait
her turn for attention. Orally, she appears to be
quite good and is very ready to answer questions.
Of course, she is an extrovert and loves to show off
in front of the rest of the class. (December 1977)

The need for attention and the extroverted behaviour must all have come from the battles she had with Mum over the years, and the way in which attention was never given to her unless it was negative or attached to conditions; I can't help but cheer little Jenny on when I read of anything in those files that shows a spark.

My own spark was something rarely ignited. As well as the cruelty over bringing animals in and out of our lives, food was another way in which power was exercised. I was always told, when we were fed, that we were very lucky and that the things we were given for dinner were absolute luxury. This would mean tinned spaghetti, but, as part of the mind games Mum revelled in, black was white, cheap was luxury and our broken little lives were charmed beyond belief when she said so. They both gave us horrible food, it was always the cheapest of the cheap, but they ate well.

As we got older, I became aware that Jenny was often sent to her room while the rest of the family ate. My brothers and I would have junk, Mum and Dad would have a different meal, but Jenny would get nothing. She was starved, literally starved. Sometimes I would sneak food to her, but I knew there would be hell to pay when I was caught. I wish I had done it more; I wish I had stood up to them and taken the repercussions. Living with it day to day was hard though. I was only a little girl and my world was toxic. Mum still barely spoke without swearing, and when Jenny was there she bore the brunt of it. 'If that bitch thinks she's getting fed tonight, she'll have a long wait,' she'd say. 'She's getting fuck all. She can lie in her own piss for all I care.'

This was a seven-year-old, a child. When Jenny lived with us, she was treated worse than an animal (although there was no kindness for any of those brought into our lives either). Mum never said a kind word to me or my big sister; I genuinely have no recollection of her ever being gentle or even neutral. It was all nasty. There were no hugs in my childhood. I have never sat in anyone's lap while they read me a story, I have never had my hair stroked as I fell asleep, I was never told I was loved or that I was special – I was just another part of their broken, twisted world. There was no softness to Mum at all; she was always barking out insults and cursing, while Dad... well, Dad was just 'there'. He had very little personality and there was no drive to him. At this point he was just a lazy, forgettable sort of man.

At the most, he would only spring into action when

Mum told him to. When he came back from fishing trips, she would tell him how awful we'd been and that he would need to discipline us for our terrible behaviour. We'd be threatened all day with his return, but being alone with Mum was a whole lot worse than Dad coming back and hitting us. 'If you cry, I'll give you something to really cry about,' she'd warn us.

She had quite a few favourite ways to make us feel terrified, but her preferred one was when she made us choose.

'Stand there,' she'd snap. 'In a line. Against the wall. Don't make a fucking sound.' We knew better than to make any noise, but we also knew what was coming. 'Right – who's getting it tonight? Which one of you little bastards is going to be first when your dad gets through the door?' It wasn't a rhetorical question; she was actually asking us, asking *us* to choose which one of us should be battered. Sometimes she would decide that I or one of my brothers or Jenny should get to make the choice alone – they could pick which one of the others would be hit; at other times she would let us all argue about it, until the weakest, or the one who had no one on their side that day, was left isolated. All the time, she would sit or stand watching us, smirking, creating her own little *Lord of the Flies* scenario where she turned child against child, waiting for us to work out who was strong, who was vulnerable, who would turn against the rest to protect themselves.

Often, when Dad got back, she'd change her mind anyway. After the horror of making us choose, she'd select another child for him to focus his violence on, or tell him that we'd all been little shits so we all deserved a good hiding. It was completely warped that we actually thought this part was unfair – after all the decision-making, after all the pitting of one sibling against the others, it just seemed so *wrong* that we all got beaten anyway. It was just a power trip for her. Four or five children, all so little, all fighting for their survival.

I would tend to sit in the corner of the living room, quietly hoping no one would notice me. It rarely made a difference. Dad hated noise, and it affected a lot of things – not only did we have to shut up, or be threatened by Mum that she would tell him if we'd been noisy, but other parts of family life that could have brought some normality were twisted by what he wanted, or she wanted, which always took priority over us. My mind seems to keep going back to the dogs that came and went. They would be there one day, then the next, they were gone. Dad threw a puppy into the road one day to punish us and we watched as it was run over, a gorgeous Labrador. It seemed that as soon as we fell in love with a puppy or dog – especially me or Ian – they would get rid of it. You learn not to love; you learn to close yourself off when you're brought up that way.

It was clear that Dad, generally, thought we were in the

way, as he was permanently annoyed by us. He'd fish and come home, and we'd be in line, waiting for the violence. You could see in his face that he saw it as an imposition on his time; it was just bloody annoying to have to batter these kids after a nice, peaceful day of fishing. But Mum would be waiting: 'She's fucking done this, she's fucking done that,' would be rattled off and, if we hadn't been forced to choose who was to be hit, she'd do the choosing, taking her time, making us sweat.

We sometimes had to choose who *wouldn't* face the hands or the bat. Ian would protect me when he could. In Jenny's absence he was the eldest, and on the rare occasions when he could wield any power he would try to look out for me, save me from it. If I was allowed to step out of line while the boys were beaten, I had to watch. I wasn't allowed to avert my eyes, and I wasn't allowed to say anything. It was a particularly effective form of torment. Those who were hit naturally felt awful, but the one who wasn't felt guilty that they were escaping it on that occasion, and there was also an odd sense of not being part of the gang. All of this meant that we were constantly trying to please; but the truth was, we couldn't – we didn't clean properly, or we made too much noise, or she'd make up something else.

The setting us against each other was relentless. When Jenny came home, she would be told what a lovely time we all had when she wasn't there – it was all lies of course, but it must have had an impact on her. To us, when Jenny was away, Mum would say that our big sister was living the high life, delighted to be away from us and pampered beyond belief where she was staying. More lies. I didn't really have any concept of where she was at any particular time, whether it was in foster care or in other accommodation, partly because I was too young to comprehend the differences, partly because of Mum painting this picture of a fabulous mansion where Jenny was treated like a princess, only deigning to come back when she felt like it. Then, on her return, she would weave a web of lies about the wonderful life the four of us had with her and Dad, and I would see such a sad look in Jenny's eyes.

I remember one time when Jenny was home from wherever she was staying, and Mum was furious for the entire visit. She had been shouting and swearing constantly, threatening Jenny the whole time, slapping her, telling her that she was nothing and that we all hated it when she was back. One day I was in the living room, trying to avoid it all, trying to make myself as invisible as possible, when I heard a commotion from the hallway. Peeking round the door so I could see what was happening on the stairs, but terrified to get involved, I saw Jenny at the top with Mum a few steps below. She was pulling one of Jenny's arms, trying to drag her down, trying to unbalance her so that she would fall down the stairs, but Dad was holding Jenny's other arm, trying to pull her back.

'I'm going to kill that little fucking bitch!' Mum was screaming. Dad, as usual, wasn't really saying much, just a vague, 'Now, now', but at least he was trying to stop her from dragging my sister down to injury, possibly even broken bones. 'Get your fucking hands off her!' Mum ranted. She was always saying Jenny was 'dirty' or 'smelly' and I know that there were constant issues with bed-wetting. The social work reports do say it was a problem, but those who cared for her when she wasn't at home did make progress. It all just regressed when she was back with us. Living in terror, constantly belittled, battered every day: is it any wonder she couldn't control the bed-wetting? I get snatches of memories flooding through from those years when I was too young to make sense of it, but already knew it wasn't right. Flashes, images that jump into my mind when I try to make sense of what Jenny's life must have been like: a snapshot of Jenny in a kitchen chair with Mum's hands round her throat, trying to choke her. Sometimes, the memories are more detailed and I recall the words as if there is a taped conversation in my head, imprinted from those awful days.

One day I heard a commotion coming from the bathroom and Dad shouting something about not going 'too far'.

'She put that radio in the fucking bath to break it on purpose,' Mum yelled back.

'But don't go too far, Lesley,' Dad repeated.

'Too fucking far? I'll drown the little bitch!' she shrieked.

And that was Jenny's life when she was with us. In later years, she told me her first memory was Mum forcing her to eat her own poo. Who knows what those three years were like before a neighbour reported Mum for beating her? Who knows what that tiny little girl suffered, what hell she went through? There are pictures of her around that age, standing on a chair, and her body is black and blue; but she's still smiling. I guess that was all she knew, just as it became all I knew.

I struggle to find anything good to say about those days, Jenny. It all seems so bleak – all I can think is that the bad things don't fully make you the person you become. They don't define you – they just make the path a little trickier, the thorns a bit more prickly. But, oh, how I wish we could have had some easier times, some happy memories. Those of us who survive should be proud of what we have been through but there is always a part that thinks, what if? What if we'd had good parents, a nice life, a chance? What if, Jenny, what if?

CHAPTER 4

WHERE THE MEMORIES BEGIN
1977–1979

We didn't have much in the way of family life – well, not in a positive sense. Ian was quite isolated, a loner who spent most of his time in his bedroom, reading a lot. I had a doll that was almost as big as me, which I loved so much, but that was about it apart from a few bits of toys. I didn't get to keep my doll for long as Mum gave it away to a friend of hers for her little girl, right in front of me. I begged her not to, but she just told me to 'shut the fuck up'.

The house was furnished with things my parents got from social services – they only had to ask and it was provided, all the furniture they needed. It was all very functional, though; just reasonably bare rooms, painted blue.

Every time Jenny wet the bed, Mum would make her

strip it, hand-wash the bedding and put her wet knickers on her head. I do feel it was often about humiliation; there are ways to deal with that sort of thing, even for parents who have little education or understanding, but ours seemed to have a natural radar for what would cause the most emotional damage.

They drank a lot, and always had flaming rows with our neighbours – Mum would punch people's front doors during her fights with them, getting furious if no one reacted, and in the morning she'd be too hungover to get up, so we'd sort ourselves out for school, even though we were all still very young. I wore second-hand clothes, and old-fashioned things like a plastic mac hat; there were no nice clothes or pretty things in my world – although none of that would have mattered anyway if I had felt loved and safe. No one ever really said anything about the state we were all in as we were recognised as the trampy family anyway, and I suspect many other kids were warned to stay away from us.

I have no idea when my own abuse started, as I can't really remember a time in my childhood when it wasn't going on. I have often wondered if anyone else was involved, as there were often unsavoury characters in the house. We would all be sent upstairs when they had one of their 'events', but it was quite obvious what was happening. I do remember – when we were in our first house, so I was no more than seven – Dad taking me to visit another man, someone who lived nearby. I know he had black curly hair that I focused on while I sat on his lap, as he tickled me and touched me under my clothes, but I don't have any memory of anything or anyone else. It might have been worse, it might have been nothing, because there is always the chance I blocked things out, given how horrific my life was about to become. I can't dwell on that sort of thing though. I can only focus on what I know to be true and factual.

Mum had spoken to me about sex from a very early age. In fact, I can't remember a time when she didn't – it was just one of her 'go-to' topics of conversation, as natural to her as telling me I was dilatory, or getting me to choose which of my siblings should be battered when Dad came back from fishing. She told me her story about how every man she had ever met had raped her, but I had no idea what that was. The word 'rape' meant nothing to me, although I knew it was something she enjoyed talking about as she returned to the subject so often, and her eyes lit up when she informed me that every man in her life couldn't keep their hands off her. She was irresistible and they were all sex-mad bastards.

'I've no one else to talk to about these things,' she would say. 'Are you listening? You'd better be.' I would nod, and try to look as if I was taking in every word, but I wasn't terribly sure of what had happened. As well as 'every' man raping her, she was sure that Dad was having an affair with each woman who crossed his path. At one point 'a blonde', as Mum put it, moved in across from us. When Mum saw this woman chiselling a hole in her front door one day, she claimed that was a signal for Dad to have sex with her. It was bizarre.

'I do everything he asks me to, you know,' she would say, 'every dirty, perverted thing you could imagine, just so that he doesn't start on you lot. He makes my life a fucking misery, but I just take it all.'

I never heard cries and I never saw a mark on her. As an adult, I am all too aware that relationships can hide a multitude of horrors behind closed doors, but there was certainly never anything I could point to and think, 'Yes, he is awful to her.' In fact, when some of the women she said Dad was having sex with turned up at our house, it looked as if she got on well with them. I would muffle my ears with a pillow as they all got more and more drunk, and louder and louder.

I need to stop here for a moment, Jenny, because this is one of the trickiest parts of all. You weren't there, you weren't there to help me – no one was – but I hope you can help me be brave now and tell the world how it all started. I do wonder. I wonder why anyone, any parent, would talk so openly about sex to a little girl – not sex as a normal, natural thing, but the detail that I was exposed to by Mum, whether it was always talking about rape, or speaking to me as if I was someone her age that she was having a gossip with. Why was that? And what did it do to me? I wonder if it laid the groundwork.

I didn't know what rape was when she told me it had happened to her so much, but I knew men wanted things, wanted things from women's bodies, and I knew this was just the way of the world. Seven years old and already thinking that; already being desensitised to it. Mum's 'talks', the way we were all treated, the violence, the psychological torture, the isolation . . . it doesn't take much to guess what came next, does it, Jenny?

And there he was. There he is. My father. At my bedroom door.

'I've got something to show you,' he said, a smile playing on his lips. He closed the door behind him and sat down next to me on the bed. I had been dozing, but as soon as the bed shifted with his weight, I scooted up, hunched my knees to my chest. Instinctively, I was wary, but I always was. Good things didn't really happen in our house. And here was the next thing. I remember it was a summer evening, the late sun was still coming in my window and I should have been playing outside, but that wasn't allowed. I had to stay in just in case my 'ill'

79

mother needed me. She would have these 'episodes' where she declared herself seriously unwell and I was required to keep watch, which meant staying indoors for hours at a time.

'Look,' he whispered, and opened a magazine he had on his lap. It was full of pictures. Pictures of naked women. It was very explicit, I know that. It wasn't 'just' women with their clothes off, it was women with their legs open, things being done to them, positions and acts that my mind couldn't even comprehend.

'Look,' he kept saying, 'look.' His eyes flitted from the pages to me, back and forth, back and forth. I had no idea what he wanted from me. Would I get into trouble for looking, or for not looking? When he didn't get a reaction from me, he started talking about them, the women in the magazines, telling me I would be like that soon. I was eight. I was so embarrassed by it – yes, that was my strongest emotion that first night. Embarrassment. I was only a little girl; I didn't want to see naked bodies. Things did go on in our house, and Mum did talk about grown-up things with me, but this was something new, and I just wanted it to stop. It was disgusting and horrific, and I didn't know how I was supposed to react – what would cause the least chance of me being hit or shouted at?

'You'll be doing all of this soon,' he told me. 'Do you like it? Do you like them? Do you like what they're doing?' I felt concerned, but I didn't know why; he didn't touch me, so it wasn't that. I guess it was just a sense of foreboding. And I certainly had no intention of *ever* doing the things he was showing me in those images. 'Not long now though!' he exclaimed. 'Yes, you'll be like that soon.'

He stayed for a while – I don't really recall how long – then he left, patting my leg and still smiling, as if we had enjoyed something nice. A touching father-and-daughter moment. My first experience of pornography, my first real exposure to what his twisted mind enjoyed.

He didn't give me any warnings that night, didn't tell me to keep it quiet – he didn't need to. I had no one. I hoped it was a one-off, but I should have known nothing he or Mum ever thought of was ever a one-off. He was back the next night, but this time there was no magazine. I know I must have been asleep when he came in, because the first thing I remember was feeling groggy but waking up because he was lifting up my nightie. I came round very quickly as he started touching me.

'No!' I shouted.

'Ssh,' he whispered, 'ssh, there's nothing to worry about.'

And then he said it.

He said the thing he would keep saying for years.

All dads do this with their little girls.

It's normal.

Everyone does it.

After this first time, the routine would become relentless

but, although I knew I didn't like it, I'm not sure at that stage I actually knew it was wrong. One morning, at breakfast, I blurted it out.

'Dad comes into my room every night.'

No one said anything, so I tried again.

'Dad comes into my room, into my bed, every night.'

Mum ignored it and so did he. That made me think nothing was wrong with it, that he was telling the truth – dads and daughters did this. I wasn't trying to tell, I was just pointing out a fact, and if they didn't react, then he must have been pointing out a fact to me as well when he told me it was normal.

As the weeks progressed, Dad did something else that was new. He spoke to me. He gave me attention. He made me feel special. And that was the key to it all. That was how he managed to carry on the abuse for years. When he first came to the bedroom of that eight-year-old, he knew I was a child who had never been loved, who had never been made to feel special. He knew that because he was one of the parents who had ensured it was the case. He used it in a way that was so cruel, and yet was so desperately needed by me. He would sit in my room for hours, every evening, and I had never, ever had that before.

He'd say such things to me, and the honest truth is, I wanted to hear some of them. I was starved of love, starved of affection, so I hung on to the nice parts.

He told me I was special.

He told me I was his queen.

He told me that, if I was chocolate, he'd eat me.

He told me that I was all that mattered.

He told me he loved me.

And then, when he had told me all of those things, all of those twisted things combined with the nice things, he would touch me. He would sit on my bed, and touch me. It didn't hurt – we were both in our pyjamas – and it was attention, it was normal, it was what daddies did with their little girls, everyone was doing it. Then, after the touching was over, he'd talk to me again. The same words, over and over.

He told me I was his queen.

He told me that, if I was chocolate, he'd eat me.

He told me that I was all that mattered.

He told me he loved me.

He told me I was special.

It would go on into the middle of the night, while Mum was in bed; but, at some point, he changed tack. Maybe the type of touching he was doing wasn't enough, maybe he had just been testing me to see what he would get away with; whatever the reason, he changed.

'If you don't want your mum to die, then you do know that this is for the best?' he would say.

I didn't want Mum to die. I knew she was often gravely ill (she wasn't), I knew she had been at death's door many times (she hadn't) and I knew I had to be a good girl (I wanted to be). One night, he took me through to their bedroom while Mum slept. With a finger to his lips, telling me to be quiet, he slowly removed her clothes.

'Look,' he said, just as he had with the magazines, 'this is what you'll look like!'

He was excited, I know that, and I was so worried that she would wake up. In retrospect, I wondered if she knew full well what was happening. Could she have slept through it? Might she have heard him, panting with the thrill of his sordid little adventure? More than once, he put me in bed beside her – she slept, he touched me and I shook with fear that I was the one who would get into trouble.

Things changed very quickly after that in the sense that he seemed almost fearless; I think he escalated the abuse to putting his fingers inside me after three or four weeks. I can remember the shock of the first time very well, but I have struggled to know how to deal with it here. I want to be honest but there is a part of me that wonders who is reading this. I know there will be kind people who will recognise that little girl and her awful life, I know some will be supportive, but I can't help but think there may be people like him too. I don't want to give them hints about what to do, how to get away with it, and neither do I want to write anything that will be exactly the sort of thing they want to read, the sort of thing they think of all the time, the sort of thing they dream of.

So, I think I have to keep it straightforward. I have to say the facts. He started by touching me, then he got bolder and started to put his fingers inside me. At that stage, even though I believed his lies about it being a perfectly normal thing to do, it didn't feel right. I knew that part of me was private and I had a sense that it was wrong for someone else to touch me there, but he reassured me all the time.

You're so special.

I could look at you all night.

It's OK, it's nice, this is nice, you like it.

This is what dads do with their little girls.

You'll thank me when you're older.

You'll be glad I showed you how to do this when you get a boyfriend.

I'm making it easier for you – you'll know just what works when you're a woman.

He never said anything nice to me when we weren't in my room; he was still the father he had always been when it was daytime, or the others were there. The further he pushed his fingers inside me, the more painful it was, but whenever I flinched, he would try to reassure me. I never screamed, I never cried. I had no voice.

I want to rush through all of this, Jenny. I don't want to dwell on those nights, so many of them, when he would come to my room. It was every night, if I'm honest, in those early days – it was as if, now he had started, he couldn't stop. I wonder, had he just been waiting? Waiting to start this? If so, what was it that he was waiting for? It hadn't been my birthday, I hadn't done anything right or wrong, I hadn't drawn attention to myself. There couldn't be any of those excuses. He made the choice that now was the right time, but I have no idea what led him to that choice at that moment. I can't go into detail of every night, because they were all the same. He would come in, talk to me, say nice things, then touch me where he shouldn't, then talk to me again. It was a pattern set from the beginning. Did he do it to you too, Jenny? Did he do it to you?

As time went on, he'd give me money – that felt worse. I didn't want to be paid for this. I didn't want to 'earn' it. He would sit on the edge of my bed, or kneel – he'd touch me and he'd touch himself. I remember seeing the ejaculate afterwards but not understanding what it was. He'd just keep telling me I was special when it happened, so very special. Sometimes he stroked my hair, always saying, 'It's OK, it's nice.' Then after ejaculating, he'd leave the room and I would be left with that *stuff* on the floor. I knew no one should see it, so I would go to the loo for paper and clean it up. It was constant.

After a while, he started to do things to me with his mouth, but I had no idea what the words were for these things, would never have known to call it oral sex. I did wonder, why in the world would he do that? What would even put such an idea into his head? He'd finish himself off or get me to touch him.

'Do you like it? Doesn't it feel good?' he'd ask, but I'd never answer him. If he asked questions and I'd said, 'No,' it'd burst the bubble and I was terrified of what the consequences might be. From the moment he started to guide my hand to where he wanted it to be, to what he wanted me to do, I just accepted it. He'd often get me to start, then he'd finish. I guess he knew what to do. I'd just lie there, trying to keep my eyes closed. He built it up, but I was too naïve to realise what he was building up to. He told me I was responsible for cleaning 'it', his penis, and that was why I had to move it back and forwards, that was part of the cleaning, but, one day, after I had started to do that, he said, 'Close your eyes.'

He hadn't told me to do that before. Even though I often did, it was my choice, when I didn't want to look at that ugly, disgusting thing in his pants.

I shook my head, still not able to bring myself to say 'No.'

'Go on, queen, close your eyes,' he said.

I assumed he wanted me to clean it until he ejaculated but, as I sat there, he took hold of my head and tried to force himself into my mouth. I coughed. Gagged. Tried to move away. He stopped. I can honestly say that I will never shake that feeling off, that first time when he tried to push it in, a sensation that's as fresh today as I write this as it was then. He tried another couple of times, but it never worked. Sometimes he would change his mind and try again, keep pushing it in, but he knew I wasn't playing along with that and I guess he didn't want to spoil his little fantasy that I was enjoying it all. He was always touching my breasts (such as they were), always touching me down there, always putting his fingers in me, also making me accept oral sex.

It impacted on everything. From that moment on, I always felt I wasn't good enough, that I was a bad girl who no one would like. I felt stupid and scared and filthy. I felt that I did everything wrong at school and at home, that the things he made me do were appalling; but I had no choice. As always, I had no choice.

There was still a lot of social services involvement throughout this time, but they had no idea what was going on in my life, in the dark, with Dad. Mum was constantly telling me I was selfish, she had made sacrifices for me, I was spoiled and I made life miserable for her, but my big sister had it a hundred times worse.

When Jenny came back, she would wet the bed constantly, no matter what the social workers were saying about her improvement away from home, and she would be subjected to the same emotional push-pull as ever. In April 1979 Jenny was collected from Frodsham, where she had been for four and a half years – I was taken along to collect her, as they were worried Jenny would be upset and thought it might settle her to see me. *'I am trying to get all concerned to normalise the situation and accept Jennifer as a normal member of the family without reminders or threats.'*

Jenny was still on the 'At Risk' register and another social worker, Mrs Stuart, was brought in to support Miss Williams, to cover her absences and to act as a further safeguard. Before Jenny went to her new school, Miss Williams met with the Head, Mr Wootton, and told him the story – they both agreed it would be a struggle to get Jenny to school not smelling, and that she would be taunted for it by the other children. Miss Williams says in the report, *'I feel Mr and Mrs Yeo are inclined to lie in and let the kids fend for themselves in the mornings.'*

Yes, that's exactly what they were 'inclined' to do. But while social services were watching Jenny, I was dealing with Dad's 'inclinations' every night. He'd force my legs open, put his penis in between my legs, then close them tight. At first he'd rub himself to orgasm, then he would enter me. It always followed a pattern – he'd take my pyjama bottoms off, talk to me, tell me loving, twisted things, then do what he wanted to do. I hated it. The pictures in his magazines were really scary to me – I knew he was doing those terrible things to me, and the images would flash through my mind. I'd try to squirm away but I was so small and his whole body pinned me down. He'd often call me Nettie after my Auntie Jeanette, grunting and saying her name over and over again. He'd leave his mess on me and the bed, meaning I had to lie in it that night and clean it up as best I could the next day.

Sometimes, the raping was very quick but it was always excruciating – I bled a lot but I couldn't tell anyone. Often, I'd throw my knickers in the bin and get into trouble for that. I'd get no sleep, either through the fear of him or him being there, but I'd still be off to school the next day, walking in pain, trying not to cry. I learned not to feel or say anything, though; I just got on with it. I had an overwhelming sense of being completely bad and completely guilty. 'This must be my fault because I am so bad,' I would think. 'Mum can't die, Dad can't leave – I have no choice.'

I bit my nails down to nothing – and Mum teased me mercilessly about it. She once made me go to school with plasters on the ends of my fingers and said I had to leave them there for weeks to make me stop biting. In normal kids, who had baths and washes, they would fall off naturally but we rarely washed so they just got dirtier and dirtier. Eventually they did fall off, and I was terrified I would get into trouble, but Mum had lost interest by then. I also had a squint in my eye that I'm convinced was related to the trauma I was going through – I don't have it any more, but it was very evident back then. I lived in a constant state of nervousness. I was the quietest of the family, according to Grandma, and I tried to keep out of the way whenever I could. At night-time that was an impossibility because he knew where to find me, but during the day, I just wanted to try and guess what would keep Mum calm so my world would be less horrific.

I often sat in the corner on my own, but that could enrage her too, so I would try to judge, try to second-guess – a habit I have to this day whenever I'm with other people. I'm always scanning a room, attempting to work out what would cause the least drama. I think it's something many survivors do; it's hard-wired into us. There were nights when I got no peace, even after Dad had left me once that night's abuse was over, because if Mum was drunk – and she was a rotten drunk – she'd often take it into her head that she wanted company, so she'd scream at me to come downstairs, where she'd be watching a Barry Manilow concert or something on TV. Often bleeding, always sore, I'd crawl out of bed, my hands feeling the damp patches on my bed, or my legs feeling sticky, or my feet touching the mess he had left on the carpet from his disgusting body, and stagger downstairs to be shouted at for nodding off, or not 'enjoying' myself more. In the morning they'd still be asleep, drunk or idle and I'd be sitting at my desk at school like a zombie, with teachers thinking I was stupid or lazy as my body and mind paid the price of what went on virtually every evening at home.

Mum's behaviour could switch very easily and there were always drinking sessions, sometimes with parties, sometimes not. These parties could go on for days and, again, I would have to navigate it all. There were usually fights, clothes thrown out of windows. Sometimes we'd be bundled out to Grandma's if it got really bad. Mum had scars on her forearm where she punched her way through a glass front door to batter someone on the other side. I definitely remember being taken away somewhere else that night. There was always someone fighting, whether there was a party or not, as Mum and Dad rarely stopped even when they were alone. Once, Mum threw an electric fire at Dad; another time she stabbed him. She was always trying to get a reaction but it was only fishing or abusing me that ever roused him.

He kept saying he loved me, I was special. So very special. I did want to be loved, of course I did, but if this was the only love I deserved, it was because I was bad. Mum was always angry with me – nothing had changed in that department. He'd say, 'Touching there is just like an arm or a leg, it's just skin, isn't it?' He was looking at my body more as it changed and I became just something for him to play with. They were both twisted and we didn't stand a chance.

While Dad abused me sexually, Mum didn't seem to

let up on Jenny psychologically. Jenny had asked Mum why she had been sent away and there was a vague story given about Mum not being well and maybe smacking her too hard so the doctors decided to separate them. When Jenny asked, 'Why only me?' Mum said it was because she loved her best and sometimes mummies hurt the child they love most. Horrible lies; horrible things to put in a child's head.

We were both learning to blame ourselves, learning that there was little we could do. As I got older, I'd try to pull away or say no, but Dad had an answer every time.

'It's better that I do this with you than another woman as that would be really wrong,' he'd say. 'I'd have to leave, and then what would happen to your mum and the boys?' Another favourite line of his was, 'I'm doing you a favour because when you get a boyfriend, you'll know what to do.' He liked that one a lot.

None of those actions were the worst things, though. The worst thing by far was the shame of the sensations feeling nice – and that haunts me. I now know it just means your body is working normally, but any nice sensations as an adult then come with guilt. This is something I feel very strongly about, and it's a part of my story I have wrestled with. I am so ashamed, but I also know that many other survivors feel the same way and it's important to let them know it isn't their fault. They're not the only ones who have this, and it's nothing to do with them being bad or dirty or shameful. Your body is simply set up to react in a certain way to certain things – it does it without understanding the context or the perpetrator; it just *does*. I hate him for that. He didn't just take my childhood, he took parts of my adult life too; he took it all when I was just eight years old. The sad truth is, I rarely considered it an option to tell him to stop. I'd been groomed since birth to be no one, nothing.

We moved quite a few times and those moves are the real markers of the different stages of my life. Not that long after the abuse began, we left for a big four-bedroomed council house that Mum had really pushed to get. I can see in the files that she was always complaining about where we lived, that it was making her life a misery, that we deserved somewhere better. Wherever she lived was never right for her though. I guess you can't leave yourself behind, no matter how many times you move to another building – you carry what is inside you and that's why everything just kept on as it was; wallpaper and more bedrooms could never alter how broken our family was.

The physical and sexual abuse continued, and I can remember it much better from that point. There are lines in my head, in my memory, depending on where we lived, and in that one, I vividly recall the constant backhanders across my face, the bleeding noses, the way she wound my dad up to batter me black and blue. Any time I tried to gather the courage to ask for something, it would be thrown back in my face. I desperately wanted to join the Brownies and finally managed to bring myself to make the terrifying request, which was immediately refused.

In terms of my grandparents, I only really had contact with Molly and Harry but there wasn't much of a real relationship with any of them. Jenny and I didn't see Ivy and Bert very much; they didn't visit us and only ever had anything to do with Ian. My mother would tell me they hated me, and that they thought I was the instigator of all the problems in our family, so I didn't go to see them. On the few occasions I did go to their house, I remember feeling as if I wasn't wanted there, so it wasn't something I was keen to do.

I think there was a deep sadness in Molly, my paternal grandma. Dad was their only child. Although they had tried to have more, sadly it wasn't meant to be. Grandma used to talk a lot about her lost babies, and sometimes she would cry. 'I had more babies, you know,' she would tell me, but I didn't really know how to react, as I was only little myself. It was very sad.

When we were small I remember sometimes going to Grandma Molly's house just round the corner from us, in the night when Mum and Dad fought. We would be bundled round there and would all be put onto the large sofa in the parlour, a room where we were never allowed normally. I would look at the ornaments (mostly of the Queen's corgis) and photos. I can still remember the smell of their house, and the movement of the big rocking chair in the back room where everyone sat. There was a dining table with a thick red table cover and, on the odd occasion us kids went there alone, we played cards with Grandma and Grandpa at that table. They used to keep 2p pieces in a tub of Steradent cleaning tablets for false teeth, or we would play for matches.

I also remember they kept a toy with magnetic numbers and letters on and it was a really special treat to be allowed to play with that. The only couple of happy memories I have of my whole childhood are from being with Molly and Harry; they were very kind people. Grandma would give us orange juice and Grandpa would rub his bristly chin on my forehead and call me 'little ears'. I think they loved us. I think so.

I stayed at their house one time and there was a chair next to the bed with a little blue torch on in case I needed to get up in the night. Their house was old, with steep stairs and extra steps to the bathroom. I remember thinking that night, 'Wow, Dad can't come in, he isn't here!' And it was quiet, so quiet, and so very warm – Grandma had tucked me in with a heavy feather quilt that felt like safety. She had lots of crystal ornaments in that bedroom and I used to pick them up one by one, really carefully, thinking I had never seen anything so beautiful.

Grandma worked in a fruit shop and if I went past she would give me an apple and I would devour it. On the rare occasions they did visit our house, they would always bring food, electric cards, phone stamp cards for my mum and dad, while Grandpa would always bring each of us a single piece of liquorice.

I only ever had one family outing, a walk along Seacombe promenade, on the Wirral, one afternoon with Molly and Harry. Mum and Dad had been fighting as usual, so Molly had taken us to their house, which was one minute from the promenade, and we all went for a walk. It was just how it should be – us kids and our grandparents – but I knew what we were going back to and there was a nervous ball in the pit of my stomach the whole time.

It's a sad fact, though, that when I was small I was always wary of Grandma and Grandpa, even though I'm thinking of them warmly now. I don't think I really wanted to go back and look at those memories because tied up in them, like with everything, is Mum. I never 'felt' like I should be scared of Molly and Harry, but my mother had told me horror stories about them both, so I knew they weren't to be trusted from her point of view. I was told Grandma had sexually abused my father and his friends, and walked naked around the house. Mum told me Molly had abused my oldest brother when they were left to care for him when Jenny was born. I was also told Grandpa had tried to rape my mother; that he was horrible and under the thumb of Grandma, and that they wanted Jenny to live with them, and would never let her see the rest of us.

So, there it is – the only people who I could have confided in, if I hadn't been groomed into silence, I wouldn't have told anyway, as I believed they were also abusers.

Around the time we moved to the four-bedroomed house, Mum really ramped up the hypochondria. Of course, I didn't know that was what it was back then; I really thought she was dying. It brought some very strange emotions to the surface. I hated what she did to me, what she did to Jenny, but she was my mother. It's very hard to break free from that, and children still want a relationship with their mum. I didn't want her to die – I just wanted her to change.

Any time I wanted to do anything, such as play outside, she would tell me I couldn't, because of her vague illnesses. If I asked to go out she would say, 'Do what you like' really nastily. This made me feel too guilty to go anywhere, as I thought she was so ill. 'You'll have to stay in and look after me,' she'd say. 'Not that you're any good at it – you're a dilatory little bitch, but I've got no one else, have I?'

I never thought to ask, 'If I'm so useless, why do you try and keep me with you in your last days?' It was just another way to control me. She would keep me out of school if she needed to go shopping. I was still a tiny little thing, but she would make me drag the full, heavy wheeled trolley up the hill to our house with one hand while pushing her by the small of the back with the other. She'd huff and puff, saying I was doing her 'no fucking good at all', and I would feel my lungs burn with the effort of pushing a grown woman and dragging the shopping along at the same time.

One night she told me it was time for her to 'go', so I would have to sleep beside her as she died.

'I'll lie here on the couch and I can only hope it'll be painless,' she said, all the while looking the picture of health. 'Don't you fucking dare fall asleep, not while I'm on my last legs. You can sit there –' she pointed to the floor – 'and if I need anything, I'll tell you.'

I did sit there, by the old-fashioned brick fireplace, and waited, exhausted, as my mother 'died'. Finally it was too much. Mum was snoring, wrapped up in blankets, and I closed my eyes.

I woke up to her screaming, 'You little fucking bitch!' and kicking me as I lay there. 'If you can't be bothered to look after me, then fuck off to your bed, go on!'

'I'm so sorry, Mum, please let me stay,' I begged, confused as always by the twisted emotions I was feeling, but knowing I couldn't bear for her to die that evening, alone, on the sofa, thinking I didn't care. 'Please, Mum, please!'

'Oh, fuck off,' she said, and stormed upstairs to her own bed. I didn't sleep a wink that night, terrified that she would be dead in the morning; but there she was the next day, large as life, and it was never mentioned again. Well, not that particular 'dying' scene, but it stuck in my mind – Mum could die at any moment, so, above anything else, I had better try to be a good girl. For both of them.

We are warriors, Jenny, all of us survivors. We are warriors and we survive for a reason. I wish I could save us, you and the little Karen, and I'm trying to do so the only way I know how, by telling our story, but even warriors get tired. At times, I am exhausted by all of this. Writing it down makes my body ache and my head throb. I want to forget it all, but only by remembering will it be our legacy. I don't want to hold on to the past any more; I'm not a victim. It has taken me a while to realise I don't need anyone else's permission to be who I am – I can decide. I have that power. So, yes, warriors get tired, but they always rise again – always.

CHAPTER 5

LEGACY
1984–1985

We moved again, when I was eleven, to a semi-detached place on a council estate. I have to admit, Mum had started to look after our places better. She was proud of this house, which was well decorated with a smart new door. In previous houses, she had never really done anything homely, and always blamed the council for us not having nice things and for the lack of luxuries, but in this house, she made more of an effort.

Mum watched a lot of TV, and she also liked the radio, so these were focal points of the living room and kitchen in every house we had. Previous houses had been full of what you would consider typical 1970s décor. There was a lot of orange and brown, with the few ornaments being glass, striped fish and a couple of wooden wall hangings.

The gaudy three-piece sofa set and net curtains of earlier houses were dumped when we moved to the new place, and the furniture and décor became a lot plainer. I think that was a general move that most families made as the technicolour horrors of the 1970s got left behind.

I don't really have memories of specific things, to be honest. Most people don't truly 'get' the monotony of an abused childhood. For me, the day-to-day worries about when my dad was going to get me, or what Mum was going to do, are there as constants now, just as they were there as constants then. I don't remember the happiness of dancing around to the charts on a Sunday evening or popping out to the ice cream van with friends during summer holidays – in fact, I'd be hard pushed to tell you what was in the charts at any given point, or even to say what my favourite ice cream flavour was. It was a childhood of joylessness, and if I was to detail every second of that, you'd soon put this book down, I'll bet! But I was living it. Of course, not every second was torment, but there was always a wariness, a watchfulness, checking to see where they were, trying to sense what the mood was, and that took away from any childhood pleasures or more innocent memories.

Irrespective of where we lived, Mum still liked to have a drink, always if she was out at a pub and often at home too. She'd take any excuse, any company, and, unfortunately it always led to trouble, whether that was fighting, kicking someone out, or trouble for me or anyone else who was around.

In high school, I had very few friends apart from one girl called Jo. She'd call for me to go to school, but never come in. I'd go to hers, though, and I thought her mum was amazing as she was always baking and was really nice to me. I'd never before seen the sort of family environment that Jo had, where people loved each other and were caring. I was welcomed and, ever since then, I've spent my life looking at families with envious eyes.

Jo's dad was actually her stepfather and he treated her really well – in fact, he treated her so well that I started to look for signs, suspicious that she was being abused too. There was nothing, though – they were genuinely just good people. Jo's family was making me think – if they were nice and normal, then maybe what I had wasn't right. I started to see holes in Dad's arguments and started to try to say no. I'd push him off – not violently – but he would change, putting his hand round my throat and pinning me down, raising his fists to me. This frightened me so much that after a couple of times I stopped saying no.

The sexual abuse was the same in that new house as it had been in the previous one – constant and horrendous. Oral, fingers, rubbing, rape, telling me I couldn't get pregnant as he'd had a vasectomy, saying 'You're not a virgin, you're tarnished, marked, people will know you're dirty.' I believed him – why wouldn't I? Mum became drinking buddies with a neighbour and was out three nights a week, and this gave him complete free rein, free access to me – until Mum put a lock on my door when I was thirteen. The fact that she did so would become a very important point in my story; it wasn't the action of a woman who suspected nothing. But still, if I left my room, he was there. He never slept. If I ran to the loo, he'd be there when I came out. I'd use a plastic tub, a Tupperware one, in my bedroom for the toilet, ashamed but desperate. If I went for a bath, he'd follow. He'd say 'Karen' over and over again outside my door in a low, menacing way. He tried every trick in the book – your mum's ill, your mum wants in. I'd go into my room and there'd be lacy underwear and candles on the bed. It was sick.

I don't think I could really comprehend how far he would go in his obsession, but there were so many signs. One day when I was thirteen I came home from school and went into my room. I had pictures on the back of my bedroom door of Michael Jackson, and I always scanned them – scanned everything, checked everything – it registered that there was something off about them that day. They just didn't seem to be aligned as they normally were. Something wasn't right. I walked over to get a closer look and saw that in one of them, for some reason, the head was separate from the rest of the poster. I removed it and was shocked to find a hole in the door, covered up by the picture. I searched and found two more. I put the pictures back and sat down on my bed, shaking. He was spying on me. He had drilled holes in the door, then put the posters back in almost the same place, leaving a slight gap so he could see through the space and watch me.

Every night after that, when I went to bed, I would use my dressing gown and my coat to cover every inch of the bedroom door so he couldn't spy on me. He just wouldn't leave me alone; I could never settle because he was always there, always trying to get me. He was often standing outside my room at night, sometimes trying to get in through force, trying to get me to open the door (which I never would, never voluntarily), or just waiting with endless patience for me to have to go to the toilet.

The lock gave me some safety, but there were occasions when he removed it or, sometimes, got to my room before me or cornered me in another part of the house. I knew Mum took sleeping tablets a lot of the time, so maybe she didn't know when he was leaving their room. I remember being forced by him into sleeping in their bed once while she was in hospital – he left at one point when he thought he heard a noise, and I heard Ian's voice. When the door opened again, I prayed that it was my brother, that he was coming to keep me safe, but it was Dad. I think Ian knew I was in there, but I also think Dad would have made excuses or threatened him to keep away.

The spyhole was just one of his many attempts to control me and get to me at every turn. One night, he cornered me in the kitchen and had his hands inside my clothes when Kev walked in – he was only nine, but he must have seen it, must have known it was wrong. Dads don't do that. Except mine did. I think the lock being put on my door had incensed him. He took every chance he could – the bathroom, any bedroom, the hallways – he followed my every move and my life was like a military operation. I moved around only where it was 'safe', where there were other people. This was it; this was every day for me now that he couldn't just come into my bedroom each night.

I went home one lunchtime and he was there. He said Mum had gone to the shop, and would be five minutes. I ran upstairs and locked myself in the bathroom because he could do a lot of damage in five minutes. I stayed there for about an hour, until one of my friends came to get me to go back to school. She was angry at me for making us late but he was even angrier with me, and said, 'Wait until I see you later.' He did see me later, and what he did to me makes me wonder why I even bothered trying to avoid it. He would always get me; he would always manage to do those things to me. Maybe it was just a basic survival instinct that made me try to avoid it when I could, even though I knew I could never really get away from him. I worried what would happen when I was older and would perhaps want to go out at night. It would be impossible for me, I knew that, because my life wasn't normal. No one protected me, no one at all.

There was one occasion when Mum walked into my bedroom in the middle of the night. Dad was standing at my bed, and she would have seen that he had no pyjama bottoms on. My nightie was pulled up and my bedclothes were pulled down. She left, he followed, and a while later she screamed, 'I want her out of my fucking house!' Later on, I walked past their bedroom and heard her say, 'She's still in her room.' He replied, 'She's probably playing with herself.' That was it, that was Mum's involvement and that was the answer she accepted.

I remember, when the lock was put on my door, thinking, 'She knows.' Certainly, once it was in place, Mum constantly screamed at me about my door being locked. She was blaming me I felt. She would say, 'Why are you in there and the door isn't locked?' The truth was, he would have been in earlier and taken it off so it wouldn't work. One night I walked downstairs, not knowing Mum was out. He held his hands out to show me the lock from my door. I grappled it from him, and he gave in just as the boys arrived. I rushed upstairs and tried quickly to put the lock back on. He came upstairs, having sent the boys outside to play, and walked over to me, grinning, as he did so often, and said, 'That's a shame – no lock on your door? You should watch yourself; anyone could come in.'

I blank some of it out, Jenny – I often do.

I've blanked out what came after he said that.

I feel that a floodgate has opened, Jenny. I feel I am telling

you things that have been locked up inside me for ever – some people know some parts, but no one has ever known it all. And over the top of it is your story. We were separated so much, denied the chance to ever become loving sisters, but we were each going through our own hell at the same time, even if not together. I wonder what would have become of us if we had been brought up in the same place? Not even with different parents – although it is a lovely thought – but there, together, would we have fought harder? Would we have been a team? It's so tempting to romanticise what could have been but, the reality is, we were dealt that hand and we had to cope.

Looking at the files, it seems the older Jenny got, the less anyone really thought she deserved recognition for all she had been through. Mum was constantly pushing and pulling, never able to break the pattern of emotional manipulation that had been there from the start. I guess for some abusers, once the child gets older they almost have to reassess their approach. If they can no longer physically abuse, they can always use psychological approaches. There is a note in the file from January 1985 to say the social worker had chatted to Mum about how Christmas had gone and about the fact that Jenny had visited. *'Mrs Yeo felt Jennifer showed off and became a little nuisance. She felt that Jennifer is only after what she can get from people. She does not want to give anything herself. Mother and daughter are so alike that they can only tolerate each other for so long.'*

This was the key to so much – whenever Jenny was seen as behaving in a certain way, it would often switch off sympathy or support from those who should always have been on her side; they would think she was frequently acting like a version of Mum. Those words in that file could have been talking about either of them. The little cruelties, what Mum did to my big sister, are there in black and white, over the years, across hundreds of pages. Petty things, point-scoring. *'Mrs Yeo told me that she didn't bother with Jennifer's birthday because Jennifer didn't remember her birthday.'*

'She felt it was time Jennifer started growing up because some day she is going to have to stand on her own feet.'

'According to Mrs Yeo, Jennifer is saying nasty things about her to Karen at school.'

It was (ironically, given Jenny's pet name from an early foster-family) a constant yo-yo – she wanted Mum, she hated Mum. She lured her back, she threw her away. How could Jenny have even hoped for any happiness with a life like that? And she'd had it from the start. The file says, *'Her mouth has always tended to let Jennifer down.'* No: her parents let her down. Mum was never the adult in her relationship with Jenny, unless it suited her. In 1985, when it was noted *'Mrs Yeo told me that she didn't bother with Jennifer's birthday because Jennifer didn't remember her birthday'*, they also reported: *'She wasn't going to make any move towards Jennifer.'* Mums shouldn't be like that. They should keep trying, not playing tit-for-tat with the emotions of their child. It shouldn't matter one bit if Jenny forgot her own birthday; she was her *mum*, and her love should have been unconditional. Instead of that, it was her hatred that knew no bounds.

When it was reported that, *'According to Mrs Yeo, Jennifer is saying nasty things about her to Karen at school,'* it wasn't parenting, it was schoolyard nonsense, and it broke my heart to read it. I can see what is behind the words when the report notes what Mum said about Christmas Day. Jenny only visited us for a little while, but even that must have been so hard for her. *'Mrs Yeo felt Jennifer showed off and became a little nuisance – no one was particularly bothered when she went home. In fact, they were more relieved.'* I was bothered, Jenny, I was, and I just wish I had screamed LET HER STAY! LET MY BIG SISTER STAY! Maybe if we had all said it, all shouted it, we could have shown Jenny that she was wanted, but there was never the strength among us to do that. *'Mother and daughter are so alike that they can only tolerate each other for so long,'* the social worker reported. It may have been true, but the story behind it shows just what Jenny was up against.

Then, in summer 1985, things changed again.

Jenny was pregnant.

She had been to the doctor and was going there the next day to discuss her plans either for a termination or keeping the child. It was felt that Jennifer needed some counselling; it was stated that she would prefer a female to talk to rather than a male [. . .] called to see Jenny; she was very nervous during the interview and at times giggled inappropriately. It appears that the boy who is the father of the child is a boy she has known for quite a time and seems to have been quite an intense relationship on the part of Jenny. She had a rather naïve opinion that he would stand by her over this issue, and she would have no problems; she was in very much of a dilemma over what action to take; she did feel that adoption was not appropriate as she did feel she could not carry a child for 9 months and then give it up. We then discussed the 2 options she faced and I gave her all the necessary information.

With regard to termination; we acknowledged that although this would appear to be the simplest solution, we discussed the emotional trauma she would go through and the guilt and other problems associated with termination.

With regard to keeping the child we were quite open in discussion re care of the child and problems that would expose Jenny to [. . .] she was rather confused and what she wanted was someone to make a definitive statement she should take one step or another; we stated time and time again that we would help her whatever her decision but we could only advise and put forward the options.

Jenny chose to keep her child. Young, with no family who would support her, *'she had the thankless task of making the decision about keeping her baby'*. A handwritten note in her file says she has travelled *'a long, hard road since her last review'*. When the social worker met with both Jenny and Mum to discuss everything, the stark summary was: *'felt both Jennifer and her mother were totally unrealistic about the position'*.

It didn't take long for my mother to decide what *she* wanted out of Jenny's pregnancy – and that was the child itself. All concerned *'counselled her and gave every support and assistance but, sadly, she was left with only one choice by her mother. You take the baby and you lose your family'*.

It's there in spindly handwriting, noted down by a social worker who is trying hard to keep her own emotions out of it, but, all these years later, I read it and I feel as if the horror is coming off the pages. My own mother did that to my own sister. Keep your baby – lose your family. A family that had given her precious little but abuse and negativity since the day she was born. Mum was always telling me she would get the baby, and Jenny would be too terrified to say no to her. I wasn't sure – I wondered if Jenny would find the strength to stand up to her (and hoped she would), for her baby's sake. '*What a choice to have to make. Jenny has always craved acceptance by her family.*' But she did it; she chose her baby, and Donna was born some time later. Mum made it difficult from the start; she made it very clear that she assumed and believed Jenny would be a terrible mother. It's there in the notes, but the brief comments made by social workers can't possibly truly represent the onslaught that Jenny must have faced.

Jenny stayed with us until the baby was born, but after ten days, she left – I wonder if that was because it took ten days for the midwife to discharge her? Was she biding her time, making plans to escape? I hope so. I hope she had that spark.

Mum was – naturally – furious.

'She's fucked off,' she shouted. 'More interested in whoring about than in her child.'

I can only guess what happened, that Jenny was found by Mum and forced to come back, as that's exactly what she did – for a few days, then . . . then Mum won, and Jenny disappeared again, but without Donna this time. 'I told you,' crowed Mum, 'off whoring!'

'*Needless to say, she left the baby with her mother. She does have access but this is fraught as, when she visits, physical contact with the baby is restricted. Still a long way to go with her relationships. Needs to be liked by all and goes to great lengths to obtain same.*'

We had Donna for fourteen months, and she was dressed immaculately by Mum. I tried to always have Donna in my room, and I would get up in the night to feed her – I was only fifteen – but it was torture, as Dad would be waiting downstairs for me when I would go to make up a bottle. He would grope me as I tried to sort things for the baby, touching me in all the places he always wanted, still saying all of those things, but I tried to just focus on my niece, to get through what he was doing so that I could meet her needs – and do all I could to keep her safe.

Jenny struggled – she was always easily led, and hung around lads who were on drugs, and now she was having her baby looked after by the very woman who had ruined her childhood, by the very woman who took great pleasure in finding new emotional brutalities to inflict whenever she could.

By September 1986, my mother was exerting control as much as she could. I can only imagine what was going on behind the scenes, but the reports all say Mum was – falsely – claiming Jenny was pregnant again and that she 'wouldn't stand for it'. Jenny was back with her boyfriend, Woody, once more, but she was being so closely monitored by everyone that they knew she was on the Pill.

The inanity of some of the reports get to me. On one hand they speak of how troubled my sister was, how much she wanted her baby back, how Mum was badmouthing her at every review that she could be bothered to attend, but also that she 'requires calculator, notepad, pencils for college as only on £3.50 pocket money'. The little things cause an ache in my heart for the life she was living, neither daughter nor mother, halfway in and out of her own world.

A handwritten letter by the social worker on 10 October 1986 speaks volumes: *'She does have access but this is fraught as when she visits, physical contact with her baby is restricted. Jenny needs to be liked by all and goes to great lengths to obtain same. Has now started at college, retaking O levels.'*

Poor, poor Jenny.

She was letting things slip, according to the Parkside children's home staff, in that she allowed 'lads' to visit, to smoke, to use POT (as they always glaringly capitalise it in the files) and to let 'noise go on'. They do agree that

Jenny has coped with considerable pressures and has done very well, especially in her exams. There are currently difficulties in observing her contract particularly in having lads around who are involved

115

in drugs. Jenny needs to involve staff to move them
and not let it go on. Jenny's access to Donna is
not satisfactory and, after lengthy discussion, we
concluded that action should be taken and Jenny
supported in her contact with Donna. We felt Jenny
needs to assert herself more positively.

But it wasn't that easy. A lifetime of being abused, of being told she was nothing, meant Jenny couldn't just decide to stand up to Mum overnight. By January 1987, Mum had applied for full custody of Donna – it's hard for me to work out in my mind whether that was to get one over on Jenny, or because she wanted another life to control, another baby to ruin. Jenny was distracted at this point as she wanted to move out of Parkside into a flat of her own, and there were many meetings and discussions looking into this. There is no doubt in my mind that Mum would have used Jenny's interest in this aspect of her life against her – while my sister was hoping for a flat to make into a home for her and Donna, Mum was going full steam ahead in trying to make sure her granddaughter would be hers legally and permanently.

Mum was pushing legal documents on her when she visited and telling her to 'sign her consent there and then', as well as having custodianship papers delivered to the council. Jenny's social worker, on the other hand, was pleading with her to get independent legal advice, rather than just listen to Mum's lawyer, and ended up asking the Social Services Department legal team to step in. They, in turn, suggested a lawyer who could help, but all the time Jenny was making plans to move into a flat with her friend, Dawn, as soon as she turned seventeen in February. Looking back, I feel she was taking her eye off the ball. I want to tell her to get Donna, get her out of Mum's clutches, and take all the help she can get to make a life for them both together. Move away if she has to, definitely cut contact with Mum – just run, really. Just run. It's like watching a storm approach and knowing you can do nothing about it. Everything was piling up, and rather than fleeing to safety, Jenny was hurtling straight for disaster.

Mum started to get annoyed at this point – although she was always annoyed – and began calling the Social Services Department, saying she was 'fed up being messed about and was prepared to put the baby "in care" if Jenny continued'. This says it all. Mum would give her granddaughter up to strangers, to the system that had failed all of us, if she didn't get her own way.

In the middle of March, it all kicked off. I can only imagine how frustrated the professionals were with Mum's behaviour; she called one morning and said she'd 'had enough. She wanted the baby removed '...*today. Mrs Yeo understood that we would probably have to put Donna with foster-parents but insisted that we remove her.*' She was throwing her toys out of the pram. I think Mum was so used to getting her own way that she couldn't quite fathom why it wasn't working in this instance. Of course, if she'd only been dealing with Jenny she would have got her way, but she was faced with an army of people who had been watching her manoeuvres for years and knew just what she was doing.

They then phoned the Family Placement Team, then Parkside, to see whether there was any way Donna could stay with Jenny. It was agreed that she could move to Clumber Lodge, on the acceptance of the nuns there, for six to eight weeks, a stay of execution. The foster placement request was cancelled. A personal application had to be made to the headquarters of the Social Services Department, who were concerned about cost, but eventually everything was agreed. Mum was waiting at the door with all of Donna's belongings packed up when they arrived to take her. When Donna and Jenny were reunited, it seems as if Jenny went into maternal mode very quickly, soothing her little girl, staying beside her until she fell asleep and asking for a buggy so she could take her out. Once at Clumber Lodge, she and the baby shared a room and Jenny was in sole charge of her.

There was a strange note from a week or so later, when the social worker went to visit Mum, that said Mum wanted it made clear to Jenny that she was the one who made her take the baby, that she was behind it. Even the social worker thinks this is odd, but I see it as Mum trying to control the narrative as always.

Within a few weeks, it is reported that Donna is taking a few steps – she wasn't walking at all when Jenny got her back – and that, when social workers watch without my sister being aware of it, she interacts really well with her baby. I assume they had to be sure she wasn't just putting it on for them. However, they also said Jenny is 'terrified that Donna will be taken off her'. This seems perfectly natural to me.

Jenny has continued to care well for her baby. Physically, she handles the baby well, bathing her each day, changing her regularly, and always having her looking lovely. Jenny tries to find interesting meals for baby to eat. Emotionally, Jenny cares for Donna well and understands the need of a baby having a one to one relationship. Jenny talks and plays with her baby, especially when she is carrying out the intimate tasks like bathing and changing. Jenny has followed her guidelines well, taking full responsibility of Donna, and carries out all the chores appertaining to looking after a baby. Jenny has been disappointed with the lack of contact from family.'
(Sister Benedicte, Head of Home, Clumber Lodge)

So, what happened, Jenny? Where did it go wrong?

From what I can tell, Mum got in touch after a while – and, who knows? Maybe this was enough to make Jenny take her eye off the ball. I only have the reports and files; obviously there is nothing written down about the visits and conversations when there was no one there to see if any bile was being poured into my sister's ear, her mothering questioned, her character assassinated. Whatever did happen, she started to fall back into hanging around 'lads'. On one occasion it is noted that she stayed out until 10:30pm with Donna, and that she was starting to lose her temper when the little girl didn't eat properly. She also started questioning whether the social workers made up things about Mum. It's clear that she must have challenged them about the physical abuse when she was little as they had to show her file photos.

Jenny thought the bruises could have been either accidental or just the photos being touched-in until she saw the one with the stripes across her bottom. She then realised that we had only told her the truth and then she told me about other incidents when she had been home on trial, including two that had occurred when she was pregnant. Jenny didn't blame her mother at all, in fact she thought that she had probably been so naughty that she had deserved it. So, even faced with hard evidence, she couldn't really accept the whole truth of the situation.

Jenny said that she was more determined than ever to bring Donna up herself and have that loving relationship with her that she obviously craves from her own mother.

She was desperate to move out of Clumber Lodge – that much is evident. She just wanted a flat and a 'normal' life; but she was asking for the moon. Just as things started moving on accommodation, the notes show *'her Mum and Dad have gone to see her, and they have been reconciled'*. Immediately, Jenny started going back home for overnight visits with Donna; she had been reeled in, yet again. Mum began going to interviews with her, saying nothing was right, pushing herself into the picture, but Jenny did eventually get a flat for her and her daughter. Who knows what involvement there was then? I can guess, as it is noted that 'Jenny is in a foul mood' quite often. By June 1987, it is noted that Donna is a *'bright, inquisitive and playful 15 months old'*. Mum is giving 'additional advice' on feeding, which is *'at variance with Health Visitor's advice, and Jenny is not confident enough to contradict. Mrs Yeo's critical attitude undermines her confidence. Jenny realises she is expected to fail. Jenny is upset at her mother's interference [. . .] however, if she stands up to her mother, Jenny is sure she will be hit.'*

Mum had started leaving messages at various offices saying she was 'concerned' about Donna, but it was a chicken-and-egg situation. There were indeed concerns, but who knows what caused Jenny to act the way she did? By August 1987, it is noted: *'we have been informed by other residents that Donna is being left, time limit not known, whilst Jenny visits a man across the road. Also a man babysitting [. . .] had been questioned in connection with a local murder. Complaints from neighbours that Jenny allows people in at all times of the night.'*

By the end of September, there has been a report that a man on drugs in the flat has knocked Donna over whilst under the influence. Pot and heroin is being used, and there is a spate of housebreakings in the local area with Jenny's friends the main suspects. Jenny is also shouting at neighbours, who want action before they do something themselves. *'Also using the fire escape and throwing tomato's* [sic] *and carrots at the old people next door. It would seem the situation has deteriorated and a week's notice to quit is needed. [One of the men] is said to be a child molester. Jenny also said she had no food for Donna – she may be feeding all the lads instead.'*

Lots of messages were left for Jenny but she had disappeared. One friend said he was *'very angry at Donna being at risk due to Jenny's alleged smack problem and that she was incapable of caring for her baby. Pointed out that Jenny has not actually been seen as incapable by the authorities.'* They chased Jenny from address to address, with no luck, and the police became involved. Even my mother was contacted. Finally, Jenny and Donna were found and sent to Parkside by the police – the next day, she apologised, but it was too late. A fostering application was made and a woman called Mrs Head was introduced as someone who could help out. *'Jenny was not happy with the placement as Mrs Head is forthright and set ground rules.'*

When you wrote wishes for your future, Jenny, you said: 'I would like to work with children or just have a nice, steady job at something I'm good at. I try to see my future but I can't think of nothing [sic] as it scares me. I can see I will always be worried about money for things and will probably struggle through my life.' You knew, didn't you? You knew that you had been written off, and that you didn't stand a chance. Donna should have been your legacy, but, instead, your life was a testament to those who had betrayed you since the day you were born. I still have this overwhelming urge to reach into our picture and drag you out – to save you. The truth is, looking back, piecing it all together, I wonder if you saved me, Jenny? I wonder if this whole process of working out what happened to you has been the making of me? Maybe I'm your legacy; maybe that's what the fates have decided for us.

A report at that time also stated:

> *...it is only when she is under pressure that she*
> *reverts back to her old habit of snapping or flying*
> *off the handle. Jenny is trying very hard to come to*
> *terms with the fact that no matter what she does or*
> *how hard she tries, it will not please her mother.*
> *She is showing great insight into this problem and*
> *as she matures, hopefully it might resolve itself.*
>
> *She is coming to terms with the fact that her*
> *family do not want anything to do with her. It does*
> *seem a tragedy that Jennifer has this attitude and*
> *that she has had to spend the majority of her life*
> *in care. It can be said* ('CAN IT?' I have written at
> the side) *that she has coped with this rejection very*
> *well indeed.*

In my life, in conjunction with all of this, Dad left when I was sixteen. He just disappeared one day, so my abuse stopped; but the after-effects didn't. His departure was so sudden but, like a great deal of what went on in our childhood, I wasn't privy to what was going on in my parents' relationship. I have never found any reason to explain his actions; nothing that's added up over the years. He just left. Mum seemed to step up her control of me when he went – and she was also building up the campaign to get Donna that had been going on since Jenny gave birth to her. In January 1987 she applied for custodianship of Donna, which was granted after Jenny signed all of the forms.

There seem to have been lots of continuing threats and 'suggestions' from Mum while she had Donna, and the files are stark again at this point, and the summary of Jenny's life devoid of much humanity:

Jenny Yeo – Homemaker File

She has been in care since the age of 2 years.

At 16 years she became pregnant; returned to live with her parents, who then had care of Donna (14.3.86), until March 1987.

9.3.87 a decision was made to reunite Jenny with her baby and transfer them both to Clumber Lodge in Formby for a period of assessment.

9.4.87 Jenny showed a lot of affection and concern towards Donna.

After Jenny requested care of Donna a short assessment period at Clumber Lodge, Formby, was arranged from March to June 1987, as she had no experience in child-rearing. Jenny obtained a tenancy from Forum Housing, however due to difficulties with other residents, she was admitted to Mrs Head, foster-parent on 30 September 1987.

Behind all of this, the battle lines were being drawn once again, between Jenny and Mum, the social services, the care team – but, this time, there was a new player in the game. Drugs were taking their toll on Jenny, and things would never be the same again. I feel so odd writing about this, because I want to be respectful to my sister. I have mentioned the files commenting about her hanging around with lads who took drugs, but it was clear by this point that she was using them a lot too. She had started to take cannabis when she was around sixteen or seventeen, I think, just when the social workers suspected she was being led astray, and, almost inevitably, this led to harder drugs until finally she became hooked on heroin.

Jenny never ever talked about her drug use in detail to me, only being adamant that she never injected, she smoked heroin instead. As time went on, if I am being very honest (and it breaks my heart to write this), she did look like a drug addict. She was very thin and she had the 'look'; you learn to recognise it. Jenny never stole to feed her habit – I guess it's kind of mixed up but she was proud of that, she was proud that she had that boundary. Even when she was in the grip of it, she kept a nice house with lots of ornaments around and lots of pictures on the walls; she even had a handmade piece of glass wall art that her partner made of the two of them with their names on and love hearts. Her garden was beautifully tidy and she was very proud of it.

Jenny always looked clean and tidy in herself, but that 'look' was obvious – you could just tell. I know she tried her very best to lead a normal life for her and for Donna, taking her to the Wirral Show every year, enjoying the rides and stalls and joining in with the thousands of people just chilling out for the afternoon. She didn't ask for much – and she never expected an amazing life. She just wanted to get by; but even that was going to prove to be a pipe dream.

CHAPTER 6

YOUR BABY,
MY BABY
1987

I remember how it all started.

'This is Graham,' Mum said. 'He wants to take you out.'

She knew I'd never say no.

So, when my mother decided it was time for me to 'meet' someone, that was that. I'm shocked when this memory hits me again, because I can hear her voice and I can see her smirking as she tells me what to do.

It was abusive from the start and it now feels like he took over where Dad left off. I knew I didn't love him but it would take nine years to get out. I didn't love Graham but I couldn't say no to him, or to anyone for that matter. I was only sixteen. I just assumed he'd expect sex and I couldn't say no, as I didn't know what that meant; it had never worked for me before. I still think I have no right to say no, actually.

Graham later told me that Mum said to him, 'You'll take my daughter out but she's a spoilt little bitch who'll do anything to get her own way, so watch yourself.' I just did what she did, did what he said. In retrospect, I think he had probably heard the way Mum spoke about me – maybe he liked that I was so young; he definitely liked that I was so malleable. He started off babysitting, but within three weeks he had told me, 'This is what will happen.' And it did. Sex was just there, in an instant – not love, not romance, just sex. He assumed I was a virgin and that he was my first. What he didn't know was that it was all a trigger for me. I would see Dad's face every time. I thought I'd be with him always and assumed this was my life now. Not long after we met, the mind games began. He would call me a slag, or be horrible to me because I was obsessive about cleaning.

I got pregnant very quickly. I had an easy nine months in a health sense. Mum told me antenatal classes were a waste of time and that she would be with me at the birth, not Graham. Did I argue? What do you think? I managed on gas and air, an eight-hour labour without a single sound. I was used to being quiet when I was in pain. But, this time, there was a reason for it – this time, I was getting my baby.

He was 9lbs 6oz.

My baby.

My little boy.

My Karl.

I was tiny, so I have no idea how I managed to have such a big lad, but I was smitten with him from the moment I set eyes on him. I'd never thought I'd be a mum, never thought I'd have such normality.

When Mum left the hospital and I was alone with Karl, I looked into his little glass cot and was filled with love. I looked at him all night, feeling that it was the first time my body had worked properly and the first time I had been any sort of human being.

'I'm going to love you so much,' I kept telling him. And I did. He had beautiful clear skin, with massive eyes, and he was such a good baby. I held his hand all day as I whispered to him about my love, about how I would never hurt him, about how we would be there for each other. My body had done something good and my baby had made me a better person. I'd never make him feel unloved.

I had lots of stitches, and Mum wouldn't help me, but I didn't care. When I got home, I sang to him all the time. I told him stories. I loved night feeds. I tried to breastfeed but Mum said, 'You can't do that when people are in my house, it's disgusting.'

I was giddy with love. Karl was my world and I never got tired, not of looking after him, not of the sleepless nights. He was actually a very good baby, although my mother always said otherwise. 'Does he ever stop fucking crying?' she'd ask, as I'd look at my snuggled-up little bundle of joy and wonder what in the world she was talking about. This was a baby who needed to be woken to be fed, he was so lazy! She criticised everything I was doing. I was feeding him wrong, I was holding him wrong, I was making a rod for my own back, I was spoiling him. I was happy to 'spoil' him, not that I think you can 'spoil' babies anyway. I think she meant I was loving him in the way a woman should love her children.

I spent all my time with Graham, Karl and Mum. Graham did provide everything we needed, but I had to make sure that any money was kept away from my mother or she'd drink us into oblivion. I was still staying in a tiny room at home, with a single bed and a cot, which lasted for about three months after Karl was born. One day, Graham came into the living room with the baby as Mum walked past with a cup of tea. She went into another room, ignoring us, so I went to make a cuppa for Graham.

Mum stormed into the room behind me.

'You can make a cup of tea for a fucking stranger, but not for your own mum!' she screamed, desperately trying to provoke a fight.

'Oh, I've had enough of this,' shouted Graham. 'I'm sick of you.'

'Well, get out of my fucking house,' she yelled back, which was her favourite saying – she used it most days.

This time, it worked. Graham left and I followed him to have a chat.

'Get the fuck back in this house!' bawled Mum as I walked out.

'I will be back,' I told her.

'No! Now! Get back now!' she roared. It was as if she couldn't wait to establish her control over me; she couldn't even stand that I would step outside for a moment to talk to my boyfriend, the father of my child. She followed us out and I was shaking like a leaf as they shouted at each other, then she went back inside, only to come flying through the door with the pram, which had Karl in it. She pushed it downhill to the gate and I ran for it and grabbed the handle while Graham went for her. I pulled him off and she tried to attack me.

'That's it, fuck off, get out!' she bellowed.

So we walked away. 'What will I do?' I asked Graham. 'I have nothing.'

'Go back – get nappies and Karl's milk, then just leave,' he told me.

The front door was still open, and the kitchen was opposite it, so I thought I could run in, grab milk, run upstairs to get nappies and then belt out again. I was in the kitchen for only seconds before Mum came in and started punching me on the side of my head, hitting me as if her life depended on it. She was screaming a barrage of abuse about how I put Graham first, not her, and that I was never to come back. She never mentioned Karl once.

I was homeless. I spent the next five days with Karl in an empty flat that Graham knew of. He sneaked me in but there was no electricity, and he had to beg his friends for money to get more nappies and milk. He came back and forth, and worked when he could. On the fifth day, Graham rang his dad, who came from Yorkshire to get us all. I'd only met his parents twice; they were nice and they looked after Karl when I let them, but I was so nervous. I was terrified of being left alone with Graham's dad just because I trusted no man. I had such dreadful boundaries – not just with my fear of what could happen to me, but also with the baby. I just thought everyone was out to hurt him and I had no idea what was appropriate. When I changed his nappy, I hated if anyone else was there as I didn't want them to see his private parts. I didn't know if you were 'allowed' to let babies have their nappies off to kick about on a blanket in the sunshine. Everything was messed up because of what Dad had done to me.

Graham's parents wanted to be normal grandparents, taking Karl for walks and showing him off, but my heart was in my mouth every time my baby was away from me, so I tried to keep him with me whenever I could. Graham and his dad didn't really get on, and I didn't realise at that point just how violent my boyfriend was – he had actually attacked his father a few times, and I was starting to see that I wasn't the only one who bore the brunt of his temper. He shouted at me a lot, telling me I was a slag, saying that I was wearing the 'wrong' clothes. There was also one occasion when he said he would kill us all by driving into a wall. His face was bright red, the veins on his forehead popping as he said it. He didn't – but he liked that threat and I always wondered if he would follow through.

I only had one friend, Julie, who I'd met while out shopping one day. She often wanted me to go out with her. Graham would then lay out the clothes he had chosen for me. They were always horrible things, completely unfashionable, as I only bought clothes for practicality, never for pleasure. In fact there were very few nights out, either with Julie or with anyone else; when he did this he was just checking that I was willing to do everything he said.

If I put make-up on, he'd say, 'Why are you doing that? Who are you going to be shagging, you slag?' and I'd be in tears. One time we went for a drink together and when we got back, he immediately said, 'Who you been sleeping with then?' We'd been together all night and I hadn't so much as looked at another man. He pulled out one of the kitchen drawers and brought out a piece of wood with lead wrapped round it. He hit the worktop next to me, screaming, shouting and saying, 'This'll be your fucking head next!' That was just how I lived, and I thought I deserved it. It was always there in the background even when he was being reasonably calm. There was mental abuse too. 'When I'm finished with you, you'll be in a nuthouse. I'll drive you crazy. Your son will hate you,' he would hiss.

The three of us had been given a council house by this point. This was another world for me, as it had three bedrooms, a garage and driveway; the garden was beautiful, there was central heating – I was delighted. However, Graham's dark side came much more to the fore once we had our own home. He was the kind of man who went to football matches for a fight and he liked to display his violent streak at home too. He'd hold me down and put a pillow over me while he told me how right he was about everything, pinning me to the ground. He was big, strong and relentless; he wanted sex every day irrespective of whether I wanted to. All I'd known of sex was with my dad – and, it turned out that when he had told me he was getting me ready for another man, he was right. Sex was something I hated; it was violent and unwanted. I'd pretend to be asleep, but Graham didn't care, and I soon accepted that this was my lot. On a couple of occasions he threatened me with knives, so I came up with idea of throwing them all on the roof one day when he was out. When he discovered that, he went ballistic.

'Never, NEVER, think that you can get the better of

me,' he snarled, holding me by the throat up against the wall. 'You understand?'

I did. I understood very quickly.

He was nice with Karl though – or, anyway, he wasn't my dad, so I thought all the things I was uncomfortable with were down to my issues. I guess I knew his behaviour was wrong, but I still accepted it. I had also folded after a few months with regards to my mother and called her (and I had been sending her money whenever I could, even though we had so little). All my life I've grieved for her, grieved for the mother I wanted her to be, and I've been desperate to know what it would be like to have a loving mother – so, I almost begged her to let me back in her life. I had been very well trained.

She acted the victim and I had to apologise; she also told me Graham would never be welcome and that she regretted ever introducing us. I regretted it too. I adored Karl, but his father was another matter. Karl gave me strength; I'd protect him through anything. I wouldn't have survived without him. He was fun and an absolutely lovely child. I told him I loved him all the time, scrimped and saved to buy him a rocking horse, told him stories constantly.

But he was witness to far too much, for far too long. Once, at nursery, Karl hit the other kids – it's what he saw, it's what he knew from home. At five, he started holding up his fist to me at home. 'I'll give it ya!' he would yell, and my heart broke that my baby had seen such things. I learned to distract him, as I could never bear to tell him off. I was with Graham until Karl was six, until I really couldn't take it any longer and I was worried about what Karl was going to turn into.

The control had been relentless, as had the violence. If I went shopping, Graham would accuse me of eyeing someone up. I was constantly accused of having affairs. I wanted a job, some independence, but when I was offered a job in a bar, it was murder. He didn't speak to me for three weeks, but he still forced me to have sex. I felt sick every time, but couldn't say no. I never confided in anyone; I was too ashamed, and I was pretty much isolated. I did take the job; however, every shift was a nightmare. Graham had grown up in the village and no one liked him. People couldn't believe I was with him. He had always been a troublemaker and fighter, and it was getting too much. I'd hinted that I wasn't happy but I was scared to push it too much. I asked for a short break and, surprisingly, he agreed – I think he believed that, if I left, I would see what I was missing and run back to him. The delusion of the oppressor is a strange thing.

I had made a new friend though – Gail. We had met a few years earlier, and she was an angel in my life, my first real friend. She changed me and made me see that I deserved a better life. I was shocked when Graham agreed to a break and went to his parents for a planned two weeks. He made me have sex in our living room before he left, and I just gritted my teeth, telling myself it would be over soon and planning for the two weeks to turn into a lifetime. When he realised the break wasn't temporary he went mad and I had two years of hell. He'd break into the house, stomp about, break things, attack me – all the while, I just kept in my mind the fact that Karl needed him to go. I started to see Graham in my baby far too often.

He would just turn up out of the blue, come upstairs, check the answerphone, go through my drawers, pull my clothes apart on me and say, 'I can have this any time I want.' He said he had people watching me – and he did. 'How come you went to bed at 2am?' he'd ask, and he'd be right; that would have been when I went to bed. One time, he smashed the glass back door. I ran into the front room, where Karl was on the couch, and Graham started hitting me, my six-year-old watching the whole time, inches away from his father punching his mother in the face.

He was quiet when he saw these things.

'Karl's going to hate you when I'm finished with you,' Graham would hiss. He'd say, 'Tell your mother to fuck off, she's a slag.' And he would. My baby would. 'Tell people at school that your mummy sleeps with a lot of men.'

He'd say that too, he'd repeat it back. There were court procedures and there were injunctions – all of which

Graham ignored, but I stood firm. I knew that I needed to do this for Karl. I never wanted Graham back not for one second – it just wasn't happening.

I think we both know why I thought it was normal, don't we, Jenny? Or, not even normal, but acceptable. I only knew nastiness and abuse. I had seen it from the day I was born, inflicted on you, inflicted on me. I was trying so hard to be a good mum, but I was only one part of Karl's life. I did love him and I never hurt him deliberately, but what damage did I do to him by staying with Graham all those years? Yes, the damage had been done to me before Karl was even born, but I so wish that I could have just broken the chains and left earlier. If Gail hadn't come into my life, I have no idea what would have happened. Those six years of Karl's life, watching all of that – was it really so very different to what we went through? He had me to love him, but he still witnessed so much horror. I may have deserved all I went through – at least, I thought I did – but he didn't. He really didn't.

When Graham turned up at Sports Day when Karl was seven, I really thought I would buckle. Thankfully, Gail was there, and when he shouted at me in front of the other mums, saying I was a slag, claiming I had destroyed his son's life, Gail stood up and challenged him. He had a go at her too but she shut him up – she was fearless – and he left. Her husband supported me too, and to this day they would happily back me up on all those years of horror. Finally I involved the police. I was covered in bruises, my eyes so swollen I could barely see, and they charged him. He pleaded guilty and walked away with a Good Behaviour Order and an injunction. He broke it a few times but nothing happened. The only thing that gave me respite was when he finally met someone else and that relationship distracted him.

Over these years, I wasn't the only one living a hellish existence. There were lots of problems for Jenny at this time too. There was illness on the part of Donna's foster carer, house allocation issues, lack of financial assistance … she didn't really stand a chance. I find the sparse notes on a case report from June 1987 so sad – they note that she was up and feeding Donna cereal early, both of them ready to face the day. She was given £43 a week allowance but thought that was a fortune as she was used to living on £12 a week, so didn't want any more help. She showed off a sunhat she had bought her daughter as well as vests for her. She had bought 'a double pearl hair ornament'. The next day she's bathing Donna when the social worker arrives, the flat is tidy and clean and she had borrowed milk from a neighbour when she ran out. Donna is feeding herself Weetabix and managing very well. *Jenny played happily with her. Donna's father is in contact and visiting the baby'* – but the next day the social worker notes that she believes Jenny and Donna's father have been drinking the previous evening, although Jenny is up and dressed and bathing Donna again when she goes round.

Graham was in my life by this point, and I think Mum was having to deal with controlling both of her daughters – a time-consuming task. By October 1987, Jenny was seeing someone called Brian who had two kids and was on probation – it was noted that Jenny got 'besotted' with various boys, and would leave Donna with Mrs H without any concern. After only a few weeks with Brian, Jenny said she wanted the three of them to move in together – she was warned she was expecting too much from such a new relationship, but she was adamant and wanted to start looking for lodgings. Not more than a week later, she found somewhere. Checks on Brian came back to show he was *'silly with his offences. Theft of soft toy and offensive weapon was a kitchen knife for protection. No suggestion he is not suitable around small children.'* It was suggested that Jenny consider adoption for Donna but she said she was 'hers' and would not be *'got rid of into care as she was'*. By December 1987, it was noted that Brian had left to live with a previous girlfriend who had a child by him and was pregnant again.

In April 1988, Mum was complaining that she was worried about Donna and was being asked to look after her a lot, although no specific incidents were mentioned. A few days later, the social workers noted that Donna hadn't been at her playschool for a few weeks, but they seemingly weren't concerned about her care. There must have been lots of messages going back and forward at this time as, in May, Jenny denied to the health visitor that she had asked Mum to have full-time care of Donna.

As I got more involved with and controlled by Graham, and had Karl, Jenny was going through her own issues. *'This girl has had traumas throughout her life,'* says a March 1989 letter from a solicitor to social services about my sister.

We understand from Miss Yeo that there was an incident with her mother in March when her mother attacked her and since that time there have been further minor incidents – i.e. her mother has returned photographs with abusive language written on them to our client. Having discussed this matter in great detail with our client we feel that any action on our part would only add fuel to the fire and unless there are any further incidents we do not propose to take this matter any further. Miss Yeo wishes to have no further contact with her mother. Our client is concerned to note that you have informed her that an anonymous phone call was made indicating that our client was leaving

her child whilst she went out drinking and that she
was cohabiting. Neither allegations are true and we
understand from Miss Yeo that you have indicated
to her that you are happy with her care of her child
and that you are not taking any further action or
becoming statutorily involved.

Jenny was an adult now, so there was less interest in her
and more of a movement towards looking at Donna's life;
but, as always, there were things they never saw, things
they couldn't have seen. I saw Mum beat Jenny to the
floor when she was seven months pregnant. I saw she had
cut all of Jenny's hair off, just as she had done to me at one
point. As I was going through a lot back then, I don't have
a sense of all the details of what happened with Donna; I
just know that I felt she was there for pretty much fourteen
months – then she was gone. I know she was actually back
and forward from different homes with Jenny, but she felt
like mine; she felt like a little girl who stayed with us. I
used to have her in my bedroom and it was lovely. All I
could think of was when I did the night feeds, cuddling
her when it was dark, singing to her – and trying to keep
her safe. Always trying to keep her safe. Keep her away
from Dad, keep her away from Mum. Protect the baby.
I would use her rocker to barricade us both in my room.
How awful and pathetic is that? I was terrified that Dad
would abuse her, and Mum would hurt her – I actually

saw evidence of the latter, as I've mentioned, when Mum threw Donna on the floor when she was one, and when she force-fed her as she had done with us.

Do you remember when we would take her out together, Jenny? Those are some of the happiest memories of my life. I adored your little girl so much, and I adored the pureness of the love between us. I remember singing 'Living Doll' to her and any songs that were about beautiful blue eyes! I didn't know that you were fighting so hard to keep her on your own, but when Mum said she'd had enough – or maybe when she realised she couldn't win over your maternal love for Donna – and that you wouldn't be back to live with us, I felt my heart would break. This, this was the worst I had ever felt, and I wondered if love would ever be straightforward for any of us.

It took me months to read the files and it took me years to put my own story together. Lives like mine, lives like Jenny's, don't follow a neat and tidy path of A, B, C; they zigzag all over the place. I would think, at some points, that I knew what had happened, but then I would get some new information and it would all change again. On top of that, the tendency of people who have been traumatised in childhood to have flashbacks, to lock other things away, means that it all comes out when it wants to; a lot of the time there is no sense of 'control' over emotions and memories. So, while some other people might like things to be tidier, life doesn't work that way. It was only in later years that I got more of the story from Jenny, and only when I was writing this book that I started to put everything together, to see my own story as well as hers.

I had a flashback to coming home from school one day and Donna was gone. 'I sent her back,' Mum coldly told me, and it broke my heart. It turned out that Jenny had come home and Mum had said, 'You can stay here if you like, but I'm having the baby, she's mine.' Jenny had been controlled throughout her pregnancy and even labour by Mum, she confided in me years after it had happened. When her waters broke, Mum asked her, 'What's happening?' Jenny said, 'You're having it!' and Mum replied, 'Well, don't be changing your mind – you've said I can have it, so no going back.' That was it, deal done, and she always used it against my sister, reminding her it was 'sorted', and that she had agreed to give her child up to the woman who had manipulated and abused her from day one of her own existence.

It was only when I got the files that I realised just how much Jenny had still been going through when she was pregnant and when Donna was so little. I think I had almost convinced myself that she had got 'out' when she was a teenager, but the truth was, the damage was so deep that she could never have managed that. Her files from October 1985 say: *'Jenny adamant that she wants her parents to look after the baby and that she does not have any feelings towards it herself so I should stop worrying about her feelings.'* It's clear that the social worker is concerned and knows there is manipulation, but Jenny had to be free to make her own choices at this point, even when those choices weren't really 'free' at all. As ever, there was only so much the authorities could do. I remember the social worker took both of us to Mothercare to get some things for Jenny and, as is evident in the files, she was embarrassed, thinking everyone was looking at her, young and pregnant, vulnerable but already facing disapproval from people who had no idea she had been through so much already in her fifteen years.

When Jenny was given a due date for the baby, Mum kicked off, perhaps because she felt that nothing had been decided yet in terms of whether she was going to 'get' the child, and said she would 'sue' if Jenny was allowed to go overdue and there was something wrong with 'it'. But the files state that all goes well: *'Jenny had a baby girl. Weighed 6lbs 13oz, to be called Donna Michelle. Jenny had an epidural injection and is well. Baby has one foot that turns in otherwise beautiful and just like Jenny. Possibly coming home today or tomorrow.'*

It was only when I got those boxes and boxes of files that

I realised other people were watching this part of the story too. The social work team had been ghosts in the narrative for so long, they had almost faded into the background. I had read their typed reports but the language was often so matter-of-fact that the dysfunctional events become normalised; however, at that point, there was a young woman who was invested in our story, in Jenny's story, and I think that in those words *beautiful and just like Jenny*, I catch a glimpse of her attachment to my sister. It touches me, it really does. There were other, real people involved in our story and I think – I hope – some of them were rooting for Jenny.

My sister didn't get out the next day with her baby as Donna wasn't feeding properly and Jenny was 'losing clots'. It must have been a terrifying time for her and the emotional upheaval would have been enormous. *'Jenny did not want to hold Donna when she was born . . . Jenny has said she doesn't love the baby but will not agree to her being adopted.'* By the time Jenny was discharged on the 20th, the social worker is obviously frustrated at Mum, who has been trying to get her own way behind the scenes and has dictated that she will be 'sharing' the baby and that Jenny can have home visits once a week. *'I felt it was rather premature to be discussing this,'* the social worker rightly notes, before going on holiday until the beginning of April. It was a crucial time and I wonder how much damage was done by the lack of supervision or regular visits at that time. The records show that other people involved in the care of Jenny and Donna during this time *'had not been informed previously'* of the history. They were *'quite annoyed'* by this.

I do wonder whether Jenny was trying to keep her distance from Donna, perhaps knowing deep down that she would never be allowed to freely mother her, make her own choices or even be left alone. By April, it was being reported that Mum claimed Jenny was *'so jealous'* of the baby. It seems, from the files, that a health visitor called Mrs Yates has a good idea about what is going on, for when she expresses concern about Mum's involvement and influence and is told that three of her other children were removed from care (a very careful use of words, I feel), she replies that *'she would probably see me in Court and again expressed annoyance at not being kept informed about the background, history etc.'*. As always, there were so many people involved, none of them seemingly knowing what the others were doing, none of them able to make the decisions that really needed to be made.

I think Jenny would have made such a good mummy if she'd been given a chance, and the right support. When I had Karl, she visited me, so proud and loving – I remember Mum dragging her out and screaming at her as I cowered with my baby in bed, but I only found out from Jenny later that our mother actually battered the life out of her in the corridor. How could either of us ever have normality when that was what we were used to? When I looked after Donna, when I had Karl, I used to indulge myself in little daydreams that we would raise our babies together – Mum and Dad never in the picture – but I'm not sure if I ever believed it would happen, because I'm not sure if I ever felt I was truly worthy of it. I needed to get there; I needed to get to the stage where I felt I deserved a good life – and I wanted to do it for Karl, if not for myself – but there was still a long path ahead, and those thorns were pricklier than ever. There was no fairytale ending in sight yet, for me or for Jenny.

CHAPTER 7

GONE
1995–2009

Before I had Karl, things had been as awful as ever with Dad – he had started making me go out with him to the shop when he wanted fags, but this was just an excuse for him to push me down an alleyway and do the usual things to me; only on these occasions, I guess he had the thrill of not knowing whether someone would catch us. This went on until I was sixteen, when, all of a sudden, he left. Mum had been going out a lot in the build-up to this, seeing other men, and she eventually threw him out.

The relief was something I can barely even describe. I think I knew he wouldn't be back, because it was my mother who had made the decision – and no one messed with her really. This wasn't something I could ever have initiated, but the fact that she had chosen to kick him out meant he would probably stay out. I only had her to deal with now – and Graham when he came on the scene.

Dad was gone for ten years while I dealt with other demons, scarred by what he had done to me and never able to stand up for myself because of it, only getting in touch again in 1995 to let us know he was getting remarried. Andrew and Kev were thrilled; me and Ian not so much. I faked it though, when Andrew and Kevin called, but as soon as I put the phone down, I knew this wouldn't be as simple as one call. They were so excited about him being back in our lives that I felt I couldn't say no – as usual. I'd just have to keep pretending. It was Dad's wife-to-be who had encouraged him to contact his children, wanting us to be one big happy family. Of course, Sandra only had his side of the story, and I didn't have the strength to tell anyone otherwise.

She called me and asked if we could all meet up. My stomach churning, I made some excuse about why it would have to be in a pub for lunch, rather than them coming to see me, but the truth was, I wanted him nowhere near Karl in any confined space. I didn't trust him at all, and I was also scared of what my reaction would be to seeing him again after all this time.

Sandra was nice and he looked happy, but he still gave me 'that' look.

'I haven't seen you for years,' he said in front of everyone, but as soon as he could, he whispered, 'You're a woman now, aren't you?' and winked. I left the pub and went home on autopilot, in turmoil, remembering it all, all of the things he had done. In my head was one question – I hadn't asked Sandra if she had any kids. I agreed to another meeting with them, a reunion just before the wedding, and she told me she had one daughter. My heart sank, and I looked at him out of the corner of my eye, knowing what he was, and wondered if he had seen Sandra's daughter as a target.

My heart was filled with dread from the moment he got back in touch, but, for eighteen months, I tried, I really did, because I wanted to keep an eye on him. From the outside, we probably looked like a perfectly normal family – but the toxic waste of the past was eating through everything. There was no way I would ever leave Karl with him and I would only visit if Sandra was there, but I felt that I was the one making things hard, that I was the one ruining the façade everyone else was so keen to maintain.

With the pressure of that, I developed an eating disorder – bulimia – that came over me almost overnight. It was as if my body was having a reaction to my dad's reappearance in my life that I couldn't control. Many people think eating disorders are about wanting to diet, or weight loss, but for me, it was nothing to do with food – it was always tied into my emotions, it was a way of escaping life and the only thing I could control. It was always worse when I was on my own or under stress. It still is. One mouthful of food can send me over the edge. There's an urge to keep being sick when I start, something switches off and I'm gone for a while. I've had a damaged stomach lining and oesophagus. I get tired and weak. I don't suppose it's something to be surprised about really; when I think back to the disgusting food, the rank meals that were served up day after day until I forced them down, it would be a miracle if I didn't have an issue with food; but actually that isn't why I have an eating disorder – it's definitely about control for me, without a doubt. I do want to stop completely. I hate it. I hate the headaches and tiredness and the feeling absolutely rotten in the days afterwards. For the first ten years of having bulimia, I'd make myself sick up to seven times a day, gorging on food, then forcing the vomit out, time after time. It has been a lot better recently, but I'm by no means over it.

Every so often, my dad would still look at me. It was all about perception versus reality. On the outside, we were a happy family and everything was fantastic; Sandra loved us. For me, it was all a sham. I felt like an empty shell. I pretended every single bit of it. Their wedding was in a registry office, and I went along with Grandma. I don't think I felt any anger, just numbness, which I tried to push out of my mind. I still felt I had no voice and I was so ashamed every time I looked at him. I felt people could see how filthy I was; that they could sense I was the slag Graham had labelled me as for years now.

After eighteen months, I couldn't do it any longer with Dad and I started to make excuses. I knew I was falling apart. I went to my GP and told him about the bulimia, but I was just sent away with a prescription for antidepressants. Mum came for a visit and goaded me the whole time.

She'd get drunk and cry about Dad, then phone one of her boyfriends, complaining I was treating her like a slave. She screamed and shouted, and in a bid to stop her constant haranguing, I brought up what Dad had done to me. Just like that. To her face. I confronted her but she wouldn't have any of it and stormed off. I couldn't carry this poison inside me a moment longer. It needed to come out.

I called Gail, who was amazing as always. She took me to her house and, that night, I told her all about the abuse as I lay on her bed, crying my eyes out. Everything poured out of me for the first time in my life. She was lovely, cuddled me and said it would all be OK. I didn't regret telling her, but I wished I had denied it all when Mum started goading me. I felt she now had a bombshell that she would be willing to drop at any moment. I was terrified of others knowing as I didn't want them to get hurt.

That day, I got a call from Mum – and all my fears were realised.

'Guess what?' she said. 'I'm telling them – tonight. I'm telling them all just what you did.' All I could think was, *I need to tell them before she does. I need to be in control of this*. I drove to the house before she got home and waited for Andy, who lived with her. As soon as he got in, I said, 'I have something important to tell you.'

His face dropped. 'Is it about Dad?'

I nodded.

'Yeah, I know what you're going to say,' he whispered. Then he cried like a baby for half an hour. I knew nothing of these memories he'd carried for years but something was breaking inside him that evening. Maybe that was the point at which some people would think I would have gone to the police, but I didn't. I believe in rehabilitation; I don't think there is any point in prison if the person doesn't change, and I didn't think Dad would change, so I did nothing. Also, I just didn't feel I had the strength.

I think he must have heard that Mum was on the rampage, that Andy and Kevin now knew, because on the outside he had changed. He had a job, he was nicely dressed, he had a lovely car and home with Sandra. His moody, quiet side had gone; he was chatty and friendly. It was confusing – was it me, I wondered? Was I the problem? He seemed like a different man. Inside I was dying and the bulimia was getting worse. Every time I saw him, it happened, it was there. I just wanted control over anything that was in me. When I put my fingers down my throat, it felt good. There was such relief afterwards, from the release, from the purging. I was soon in the grip of it. Any triggers at all would make me want to vomit. It was an escape from my own head; bingeing was the switch, purging had to go with it.

I astounded myself with what I ate. Three packets of biscuits, six packets of crisps and a loaf of bread, just to start with. I couldn't be any fuller. I'd eat that quantity three times over and I would do it up to seven times a day. I was obsessed. I'd take Karl to school, then run back home so I could get started. I couldn't sleep, I was exhausted and I felt so, so weak. I had no health problems for ages, though, but eventually the acid damaged my oesophagus, my stomach lining was hurt, I was bleeding, even the skin on my hands was hardened from shoving them down my throat.

At the time, there were also a lot of issues with Jenny's daughter. As Donna got older, Mum started working on her to twist her mind against Jenny. It worked and Donna left their home to stay with her. However, the novelty on Mum's part soon wore off and, when Donna was sixteen, she kicked her out to stay in a hostel. Her relationship with Jenny never recovered. It's not my place to tell that story, but all I do know for sure is that Jenny was heartbroken.

From 2004 Jenny and I started to spend a lot of time together, and I was so glad of that. She told me that when she got her first flat, Dad was round there within the first few days, trying to have sex with her, so I guess it was something he just felt entitled to. 'I'm not your real dad anyway,' he said to her, 'so it doesn't matter.' It hadn't mattered to him with me either, though. Real dad or not, blood or not, he just saw his daughters as something to be used.

I don't suppose we saw each other constantly but those were important times. Mum tried to control it, but she started to lose some of that power as I got older. Previously, if she was talking to Jenny then the rest of us were allowed to and if not, then we weren't. I remember one day we all went for a walk. Jenny and I tried to get ahead of Mum as we never got the chance to talk alone, and we said to one another how lovely it would be if we could spend time together, just us – but that wasn't allowed under Mum's rule.

When I got older and started college, I would sneak off to Jenny's flat to see her and Donna. She had a nice place, decorated just like her personality – quirky and warm. She had good friends there and I think she was happy. I know she drank with her boyfriend sometimes, but I never saw any signs of things getting out of control. On the contrary, I thought she was doing well. I hid my trips from Mum, as I'd been told I'd be disowned if I talked to Jenny – I was still so psychologically bound to my mother by the years of mental abuse, that I couldn't see that being disowned would actually be a positive thing.

Once I moved, when Karl was three months old, I saw Jenny a lot less. I was driving by then, so when I went back to Merseyside I would sometimes go to her flat. Once Ian and I took her for a pub lunch when he was home from the US, where he was living. She was so happy that day. It was a lovely experience, just me, Ian, Jenny and Donna. She had a German shepherd dog by that time, that she adored, and Donna was a happy little thing, always smiling. She was making a home; a real home.

One time, when I came to visit her in my car, she had been watching me from the window. When I got there, she said, 'Look at you, driving! I'm the big sister, I should be doing that.' There was a sadness in her voice, and she seemed to think for a moment, then quietly added, 'One day, I'm going to be a proper big sister to you.' At the time, I thought it was a sweet thing to say. Now, it breaks my heart.

I also saw her occasionally at Mum's house, but those were never good times as there were still issues of control and manipulation. One Christmas, the whole family was told to come and have lunch together, but Jenny was only allowed to be there in the evening – and it was made very clear to her that was the case. She was still being singled out and treated differently. She was told what hours she could come for, only after the rest of us had eaten, and that if she wanted to drink anything she had to bring it herself, even though the rest of us didn't get given such restrictions. It was awful for her; always the black sheep, always made to feel like an outsider.

On another occasion, she was 'allowed' to go to Mum's house after we had all had dinner, then Mum said we should go to the pub. 'Not you though,' she told Jenny. She took it all, always craving love, always willing to take the dregs she was offered. She would say such nice things, never a bad word about anyone. My sister kept her good soul despite everything.

By the early 2000s, I had a new partner, a wonderful man called Elroy who only ever treated me with respect and love. It was hard for me to trust a man, but Elroy worked hard and recognised what I had been through, and together we built the relationship I never thought I would have. In 2003, we moved to Spain, trying to build a life away from all the demons in the UK, but we did return briefly at one point. At the time I wasn't happy about returning, but now I am so glad I did. During the year we were back, I saw Jenny more than ever. I was so touched the first time I went back to her flat and saw a photo of me on her fridge. She also had an article about me cut out and pinned up from a 'Posh Spice' lookalike newspaper piece I had done. We laughed about it, but Donna told me her mum was really proud of me and showed it to everyone, saying, 'That's my little sister!'

I also bumped into her quite often and I thought she was growing in strength. We were both older and she had cut away from Mum, which did her a power of good. She had a clear plan for how she was going to get clean of drugs and I thought it was a good one, a decent approach. I think it might have worked – I really do, if only she'd had the opportunity to put it in place. We talked a lot about our past in those chats, often standing in the street for hours on end. She would say to me, 'Do you feel embarrassed if your friends see you talking to me?' and that broke my heart. I was never embarrassed by her, never. These were the chats when she told me about coming home when she was nine years old, alone, back when social services thought that was acceptable. Mum would open the door and say, 'The other kids don't want you here' and close the door in her face. Mum would tell us Jenny was having far too much fun doing other things in the children's home to want to come back to us, and that she only came when it was her birthday or Christmas to see what she could get, then she would leave through her own choice. I believed this back then, and Jenny believed that we didn't want her.

She told me she just wanted Mum to love her and she also told me about Dad going to her flat and abusing her. I had known it was true when she first said it – of course I had – but she had been called a liar when she told our mother. She cried most when she spoke about, all through her childhood, the desperate wish to come home but knowing we 'hated' her, also knowing that was impossible. It was all so cruel and twisted.

This is the part I never wanted to write, Jenny. I find this harder than all of the rest put together. We managed two years together, two years of confiding in each other, loving each other, laughing together, then . . . then you died. In August 2006, my big sister left the world that had been so cruel to her, for ever. Your spirit was incredible and, despite what you went through, you never had a bad word to say about anyone. You had such loyalty and, despite it all, you loved your family. But heroin doesn't care about any of that. It comes in, offers some respite, offers a bit of relief from all the troubles and then drags you down further and further, until there is nothing left. There was nothing left of you, nothing left for you, Jenny. I wasn't enough – I couldn't keep you here. After all you had been through, it was time for you to go. My big sister. My darling Jenny.

It was Mum who told me. A cold, hard phone call.

'I've got bad news. Your sister's dead.'

It was the early hours of 6 August 2006. A brain aneurysm, at home, without me beside her. The last part breaks my heart more than anything. Jenny had always suffered from terrible headaches but she'd never been diagnosed with anything. That night, that awful night, she started to fit and her partner called an ambulance. She died at the hospital. She never recovered, she just left us. She'd been due to go to the Wirral Show with Donna that day, the show she always took her to, the show that was their annual outing.

I wasn't even allowed to go to the hospital when I got the news from Mum as Jenny's body was rushed straight to the coroner for toxicology tests.

I was in a sort of limbo after that and all of the memories shudder about in my mind, as if they don't want to settle. They flit from one thing to another – the trip to Mum's house to meet up with my brothers, to see if we could be some sort of family. There was a houseful of people. I probably couldn't even say who was there really; I was in shock. 'Christ,' Mum said, as soon as Elroy and I walked in, 'they're going to have eaten all my fucking bread soon, the amount of toast they're making. And I'll have no cigs left.'

There were no tears. Not from her.

Donna was naturally distraught that day and I suffered what I now know was an anxiety attack. I was spinning, light-headed and couldn't breathe properly; this lasted for hours and hours. I couldn't believe Jenny had gone. She had a plan! It wasn't fair, it wasn't right. I kept saying those words to myself, 'She had a plan, she had a plan.'

***

The next time I saw Jenny was at the funeral home over a week later. She hadn't been dressed and was in a gown. Her own clothes had been laid on top of her with her jewellery laid on top of those. This was horrific; I didn't expect her to look the way she did.

'Why isn't her hair brushed?' I asked the woman in charge. 'Why doesn't she have her own clothes on?'

'I'm so sorry,' she told me, 'I'll see to it for your next visit.'

She was true to her word and, the following day, Jenny had her hair styled and some make-up on, and was dressed in her own clothes and wearing her jewellery. She had her perfume and her phone in the coffin with her (the things she adored) and I put in a letter I had written to her; I read it to her, then put it into an envelope. I don't want to share that. I want some things to be just between us.

The funeral was horrendous, but not for the reasons you might expect. Mum was on one side, with what I was sure was a smirk on her face, and us on the other, with Jenny's friends at the back. Mum didn't shed a tear, just twiddled her hair as if she was bored. Elroy said she looked cold as ice.

The minister had asked for stories about Jenny he could tell in his eulogy and it was clear, when he spoke, that he had been forced to try to repair some of the damage done by what Mum had said.

'Jenny put a radio in the bath once,' he said, trying to

smile, 'and I know that her mum felt she liked her own way, but I think we need to remember her spirit. Let us recall the real sense of Jenny. Both she and Karen, her little sister, once had dresses the same. Karen's had long sleeves and Jenny's didn't – so Jenny chopped Karen's sleeves off.' I could imagine Mum telling him that she did it out of spite, but the minister did what he could with the story. He took a deep breath and smiled at me from the pulpit. 'I'd imagine that Jenny just wanted to look exactly the same as her little sister,' he suggested, kindly.

In 2006, just after Jenny had died, Mum found out about my bulimia and she told anyone who would listen. I was so ashamed, and I still am ashamed that I sometimes do it. She had a pattern that she always stuck to when there was anything she could get sympathy for – she'd go around pubs and say to people, 'Buy me a vodka and I'll tell you something you just won't believe.' It was all about her, always. In one pub, she repeatedly told people she was dying of cancer. It got her a lot of drinks, but I guess she must have had to find a new haunt when her 'terminal' cancer never actually finished her off. I got calls about that from regulars, people who knew our family. They'd ring me up and say how awful it was that Mum was dying, and that I as her daughter needed to step up to the plate in her final months. It took me back to what Dad used to say to me – 'If you tell anyone, your mum will die, she won't be able to take it.' It was all my fault again (and Mum was telling me at this point that she *was* dying); it was all laid at my door.

Life just went on for a while but I couldn't stop thinking about Jenny and turning it all over in my mind. I kept coming back to the fact that I didn't really know her whole story; I only had bits of it from other people. I'm not sure what I expected to get back when I applied for my files in 2009, but I did want to know Jenny's story as much as my own. I knew there would be parts of the documents that would be blanked out – they say this is to protect the privacy of others – but two things really hit me. The first was the completely haphazard way it had all been thrown together, some pages duplicated, some missing, some fuzzy where they had been taken out of the photocopier too soon. They were all in a random order, and it felt so uncaring somehow – I know I shouldn't let my imagination run away with me, but it was almost as if the person doing it just couldn't be bothered. The second thing that had a huge effect was the first page of my file. On it, on that single page, was a summary. This was it in its entirety – this is what they thought mattered:

14 January 1970 – Mr and Mrs Yeo married
    16 August 1971 – Karen and Jenny placed with foster-carers while Mrs Yeo was hospitalised
    20 August 1971 – due to hospitalisation of the

foster-mother, Karen and Jennifer transferred to separate foster-parents

3 September 1971 – all 3 children returned to their parents' care

5 June 1977 – social worker brought Jenny for a visit and took all the children to New Brighton and Vale Park

4 January 1978 – social worker took the children to see the pantomime, Mother Goose

30 August 1978 – outing with social worker, picnic at the sand hills

29 September 1978 – social worker took children and Jenny for a picnic in Bidston Woods

6 April 1979 – social worker took Karen and her mother to bring Jennifer home from Frodsham

29 October 1979 social worker talked to children about stealing

I can't believe a life, so many lives, can be summarised in so few words, Jenny, but I also know that we were just a case file. Am I angry that we were never 'saved', am I bitter? I have been. That's the truth; I have been. However, I've had to move past that – do I wish someone had said 'sorry', even just once? Yes, I do – but I want it to come from our parents, our mum, my dad. They did the real damage, they wrecked our two little lives.

As a mother, I still find it utterly incomprehensible that anyone could choose to do any of that to a child – and that they could just go on with their own lives. So, this is why I need to make your story known, Jenny, this is why I need to shout out loud for all of us who have been through similar things and who *can* still have a voice. We're going nowhere. We're here, we're still standing and we will be heard.

CHAPTER 8

HER NAME WAS JENNY
2010–2011

I'd felt confused about my shame and my guilty feelings for so long that they seemed almost natural. I often felt depressed and low, and I found it hard to unpack things – I didn't know if I was naturally that way and it made the memories of the abuse worse, or if the memories of the abuse brought the depression. I'd certainly felt every emotion since going to the police about what happened to me as a child. I had felt afraid, angry, sad, confused and so very, very dejected, but, through seeing a support worker, I'd started to accept that what happened to me needed to be punished. Someone *did* need to say 'sorry'.

In the past, whenever I thought about reporting my childhood abuse, the one thing that bothered me was whether my silence was putting others in danger – was

Dad still doing it? Were there children out there who I could help by speaking out? When I finally did report it, it was because of this – I could maybe stop him if he was still doing it, or I could support others who had been victims too. It was only once I started seeing the support worker, Vicky, that I acknowledged myself in all of this. She made me see that what he did needed to be recognised, and that he should be held accountable and punished – for what he did to *me*. That was a revelation – my self-esteem had been at rock bottom for years and I had never really thought I deserved anything but bad stuff, but now someone was telling me I actually mattered.

I thought I would do this alone at first; I believed it was my problem and there was no need to involve anyone else. Even Elroy didn't know I was going to the police station, on that first day. I had driven there three times already, but on each occasion I drove away again without going in. I honestly thought I would never find the courage to do it; if you had asked me only a couple of months ago if I would ever report my dad for what he did to me, I would have said, *I'm not strong enough*. This is, I guess, the power of grooming. He did such a good job on me that I always felt completely worthless and unimportant. He was probably confident that I would never tell. I have never valued myself, and how it affected my life never seemed important.

However, I soon realised the police needed to talk to

my mother and my brothers. I was unhappy about this at first, as I didn't want anyone else to be hurt, but now I know that wasn't my fault; it wasn't my guilt to bear as to whether they would, or may, feel hurt. It was his fault. I couldn't protect anyone from this, and it wasn't my job to do so.

So, I gave the statement – all twelve pages of it – and I went home, and I waited. It was surreal. I had done this huge thing, and I knew the world was about to blow up, but there was a quietness to the waiting that made it all seem otherworldly. I spoke to Jenny in my mind a lot during those times, and I so wished she had been there to walk this path beside me.

Then the quietness ended, and the world changed. Dad was arrested on 10 November 2010. He gave a 'no comment' interview, which the police said they saw as an indication of guilt, and was bailed until January. During this time the statements went to the Crown Prosecution Service, who took just forty-eight hours to decide to charge him. He was to face twenty-four counts under ten charges, including five of indecent assault on a child under fourteen, and five counts of rape of a child under sixteen. The fact they had decided so quickly, and that they had chosen those counts, gave me a little hope. I had heard so much about the CPS rejecting 'historical' cases and I knew they would only go ahead if they thought a prosecution had a chance of being successful.

Throughout all of this, I had been having the most horrendous tummy pains. I had suffered for years, but they had certainly got worse during the period of deciding to tell the police and then waiting for Dad to be arrested. Two weeks after they arrested him, I underwent an operation to find out what was going on. Part of me wondered whether the years of abuse, or the years of eating disorders, had caused some harm, but it was discovered that I had blocked Fallopian tubes. My dreams of having another baby were shattered instantly. I had only just reached a point in my life where I could have faced having more children, and now the chance had been cruelly snatched away from me. I had honestly thought up to that point that another baby was an option and I could live with my demons, be the sort of mum I had always wanted to be and be free of my own mother's control. I could live with my feelings of distrust of other people around my child, but now this? I was told that my only chance would be IVF, which I would have to self-fund due to my age and already having a child. I felt so sad, so heartbroken, and I felt that he had taken something else away from me.

'He just can't stop wrecking my life, can he?' I cried to Elroy. 'I know he's done this – I know what he did to me as a child means that I'm broken now.'

As always, Elroy was my rock. He held me and comforted me as he said, 'It's fine, it's fine – we'll save, we'll get the money together for IVF, we can do this.'

I hoped so, I really did.

On top of everything else, my grandma was very poorly and fading fast. She didn't know what was going on, that I had accused Dad of this terrible thing. Before every visit, I had to call and make sure no one was with her, make sure *he* wasn't with her, and that system worked well until I turned up a few days into the New Year to see him there. It was a split second between me turning the corner into the doorway of her room, seeing him and turning away. Thankfully he didn't notice me, but I felt as if I'd been punched in the stomach. I walked out quickly, shaking, and sat in my car down the road, and after about ten minutes I saw him walking towards the train station. He lit a cigarette and looked like he didn't have a care in the world.

Despite Grandma being ill, the festive period had been lovely, but we were all waiting for 11 January as we knew he would be charged on that day. The worry of that never left me. I constantly wondered if he would admit his guilt and put an easier end to this for me. If not, I would face a trial; I would face being questioned. I would be put through as much as he would – was there any chance he would spare me that? All I could hope was that he would finally act as a father, that he would finally try to protect me from something. In my heart, I knew everything I had said was the truth and if I stood by that, how could I not stay strong? Sometimes, though, that was easy to say but inside I felt distraught.

The date came and I waited all day to hear what had happened. I was living on my nerves the whole time, hoping the phone would ring, dreading that the phone would ring. Finally, at 8.30pm, it did. I knew. I just knew this was it.

It was Kerry, one of the support team, and from the tone of her voice, it was clear this wasn't over.

'He isn't taking it well,' she told me. 'He's drunk and he says he's going to kill himself. One minute he's saying to your brother that lies are being told about him and he can't deal with no one believing him, then he's saying he can't live with the guilt of what he has done and he can't go to prison and live that life.'

'Do the police know this?' I asked.

'No – they can't get hold of him,' she said. 'This is all coming from him knowing that you have made the accusation. I don't know what we do now.'

All I could think was to call the police; they had been so good to me that I could only hope they would be able to sort this out. When I informed them of what Kerry had told me, they said Dad hadn't answered his bail and a warrant was out for his arrest. They sent a squad car to his home address and gained entry, but he wasn't there. At the same time as the police officers were at his house, another squad car picked him up in Leeds town centre, roaring drunk with an injury to his head. He was taken to hospital overnight to be checked – and the next afternoon he was taken to Birkenhead Custody suite to be charged.

After being held there overnight, he was moved to Liverpool Magistrates the next morning. During those two days, several calls assured me that, as he had skipped bail and threatened to kill himself, he would be remanded, but when I learned that he wanted to kill himself I just fell apart. I was devastated, because I knew this would mean he would never admit what he did or be told by a judge, 'You did this.' I would never have my closure. He'd kill himself before any trial happened; I'd never get a chance to see him punished for everything or to get an apology.

I had realised over the past three months that I needed this; I did need him to be told what he did was wrong – and I deserved it. I shouldn't care how much time he might have to serve in prison. I needed to know he would be stopped from hurting anyone else and that he would be made accountable for what he did to me. That would be enough.

I didn't sleep at all those two nights and, by morning, I had realised that if he had managed to kill himself he would have left me with one more thing – guilt. However wrong and misguided that would be, I would have felt it. I needed to work on these feelings, for me, for my sanity. I received a call late that night informing me that he had been remanded and would be kept in prison until his trial, and I wondered – did that mean he wouldn't be able to commit suicide? If he was being watched, maybe he'd have to face up to what he had done after all.

This helped me so much and the next day I felt amazingly calm. I felt that this turn of events was right and it sort of made sense. Later that day, I had a strange feeling that I couldn't quite place. I started to think that maybe it was freedom – I'd never had it before. For the first time ever, I thought I would rather be in my shoes than his. It felt . . . appropriate. I realised, right at that moment, the importance of someone being punished for the bad things they have done, the importance for their victim. And I would be a victim no more.

Sadly, the feeling didn't last.

The following morning, I received a call saying Dad had been granted bail and was free. He had even been given a lift back to Leeds. How could this be? How could he be so supported, so enabled? He had skipped bail and threatened to kill himself, but he was now free to walk the streets again, to live in his own house, to have his life back? He claimed he didn't answer bail as he had a cut on his head, and was promising to make no more suicide threats, and this was all believed.

I had so many questions, beginning with why was I told he was on remand when he was free? This turn of events knocked me for six and the next few days went by in a haze. What would happen? Would he face up to his crimes in court? Would he kill himself? I was left in limbo wondering what would happen and it all felt so wrong, so unfair. Worse still, everywhere I went, I saw him; every man I saw in his age group with silver hair was him. It was making me a wreck and I started to stay indoors. I felt weak and that his rights were more important than mine – as always; I was told by the police that he had bail conditions not to contact me and to visit the police station once a week, but it wasn't enough to calm me down. I felt that he could turn up any moment, or that he could kill himself. I was starting to doubt all of this – starting to doubt myself.

Soon, I was told Dad had been bailed until the end of January, when he would have to enter a plea. At least then I would know if he was going to admit it and save me a trial, or whether he intended to plead 'not guilty' and make me go through it all in court. Vicky came to see me every week and helped me so much to get things straight and right in my head. I know she was trying her best to make me strong and aid my recovery but she also had to tell me the facts.

The main one was that 31 January was just a preliminary hearing, to sort out dates and administrative matters, and his actual plea hearing was scheduled for 11 May. I could hardly believe it! I'd thought I just had to get through the following two weeks, stay strong for that length of time, but I had no idea how I would manage four months.

Unless you have been in that sort of situation, I don't think you can imagine the effect on every aspect of your life. I couldn't sleep, but I was exhausted. All of my old eating problems came back. I was shaking, having panic attacks. My mind was never settled. I was getting through life on a thread. There was no relief from it. Even when I did finally drop off, I would have nightmares. When I left the house, I was still seeing him in the face of every old man I passed. And I now had months of this ahead of me. It's all very well to tell someone to relax, to forget about it until it happens, but that can't actually be done – there is absolutely no escape.

Witness letters had gone out confirming the new date and I was told he had to attend the police station every day rather than just once a week, but this turned out to be another error.

'You're doing really well,' Vicky told me. 'Other people might have given up with all of this.' She had no idea how close I was to giving up too, no idea at all. I knew some people in the family felt sorry for him and were telling him to stay strong and some were telling him to keep his head down and take his punishment, then get on with the rest of his life. I wished it was that easy for me.

Finally, 31 January arrived and the trial date was set – with more potential delays, as if he pleaded not guilty it wouldn't be until 20 June. Dad had been breaching bail by contacting family members and I was told this information would be passed on. I was finding it hard to function by that point – I felt so low – but I was trying to carry on. I wanted to get back into my studies but couldn't concentrate. I had to stay strong. It all had such an effect on my relationship; Elroy was trying to be patient with me but it can't have been easy for him. He didn't really understand, and we also had the added pressure of saving for IVF. I had to find a reason to get up every day and it was really Karl who gave me that reason – if it hadn't been for him, I have no idea how much worse I would have been.

Jenny, this is tough – I had a visit with Vicky today and we spoke about you a lot. I was close to tears the whole time and I feel so cross with myself – I want to find strength, I want to be able to fight all of this, but it's as if I've been battered down so hard that I don't know if I can keep getting up. I think everything is taking its toll now. We spoke about you and your records and she tried to stop me feeling I'm wrong for doing all of this. I can't stop thinking about Mum saying, 'Look what you've done now.' And, 'When will you stop?' I know these feelings are not right and I will fight them. It's not my fault if he goes to prison; it's his own fault.

We talked about how important the social services

records will be in court. I hear that some family members will not be giving statements in support of me as Dad's feelings are more important to them. I feel so sad, let down and disappointed, I am struggling to understand but maybe I never will. How much harder will this get? Karl gets me through a lot, as he needs his mum, but you get me through too. The memory of you pushes me on – even if I feel it's reaching a point where I'm not sure if it's worth it for me, it will always be worth it for you. You can't be there to tell everyone what he did to you, but if he is found guilty, then we both know that will be some form of justice.

Things were quite stable for a bit and I almost got used to feeling scared and anxious all the time, but I knew the plea hearing was coming on 11 May and, if he said 'Not guilty', the trial would be 20 June. I was having very unsettled dreams, which may have been because, by now, I had all of my files and all of Jenny's files in my house. The reality of our childhood was starting to slowly sink in, what we went through and the basic needs that were never met; we were so emotionally abused. A little girl who dealt with all of this on top of what her father was doing to her – that's me, that's who I am. I was starting to see the person they'd made – so mixed up, and with no confidence in herself or her abilities. I was looking more and more into every aspect of my past and I guess it all went hand in hand with the possibility of a trial. I was remembering the lies told to me by Mum, and starting to realise just how far it all went. I couldn't get my sister out of my mind – Jenny was rejected and hurt her entire life; there was never once a let-up or reprieve for her. This broke my heart.

The police knew I had the files and, at the end of March, they asked me if there was anything relevant in them. I knew Dad had attacked Jenny when she was sixteen, as she had told me, and I also remembered her telling Mum, who said she was a liar and a troublemaker. But I knew she was telling the truth. He denied everything, of course, but how could Mum say we were lying when this was two years after she found him in my room? I thought the files would show what kind of people they were. I hoped so, but the task of reading them all weighed heavily upon me. More than anything, I wanted one day to feel like a normal person with normal thoughts and no demons.

I was having lots of sleepless and disrupted nights, with bad dreams and flashbacks. I'd also decided not to see the counsellor again as I had been told that this might be viewed negatively by the defence; they could use it against me to suggest my memories had been encouraged or even planted. Counselling had been so valuable to me and I knew it could help me to change my negative thinking patterns, but I couldn't risk it being used against me. I felt emotionally overloaded, but I couldn't let what had happened to me take any more away. I felt that I might have a lot to give others who were dealing with or who had come through what I'd experienced, and I wondered if, when it was all over (what a wonderful thought!), I could maybe help others by becoming a counsellor myself.

I did take medication, which helped, and I was glad that I had something to kind of numb my feelings and emotions while everything dragged on. Every day seemed to bring something else – one day Kevin got drunk and went to Mum's house to tell her he and Andy were also abused. This floored everyone. He called me, crying, saying he had remembered. He said awful things happened to him, and he didn't feel like a man any more. After he'd hung up I spent the night wide-awake, wondering, was there anything I should have done? Or seen? Or said? I felt so guilty at that point – more guilt! – for my brothers and devastated at what they had been through. Kev went on a two-day bender after his revelation, and when I went to see Andy to try and talk to him, it was so difficult to bring up. No one else believed Kev but I didn't think anyone would make it up; how could I, of all people think that? Andy insisted it hadn't happened to him – but I lied about it not happening for years, didn't I? Unfortunately, when Kev sobered up he denied saying any of it.

Over the next few days, I felt it all physically – I was so drained, emotionally and bodily. As Dad's plea date came nearer my arms and legs were sore, I couldn't sleep, I had bad dreams, my head was everywhere. I noticed a bald patch on my head and my hair started to come out. This had happened with the stress of leaving Karl's dad too. I was so frightened at the court case coming up. I was afraid of walking into a court and having someone make out that I was a liar; everything terrified me and I kept playing awful scenarios in my mind. I was told that, even if the jury believed he was guilty, they might still give a not guilty verdict. Human nature can make people wonder, 'Can I send an old man to jail?' This sounded crazy to me but I had to be prepared for any outcome; people kept telling me he would be found guilty but I couldn't assume anything. I didn't even care if he wasn't sent to prison; I just needed him to be made accountable for what he did. I needed a judge to tell him, 'You did this.'

Every time the phone rang, I thought it would be someone telling me Dad had killed himself, but it didn't happen and the plea hearing was set for 10.30am on 11 May. Unsurprisingly, I got no sleep that night and my stomach was churning from the moment I got up. This was it. Today, I would find out if I had to face a court case or if my dad would end this for me and plead guilty. Every time I thought of the word 'Dad', I wanted to be sick. I hated that he was that to me, I hated that he was part of me. I couldn't sit down but I felt weak-legged when I walked around. Elroy was finding it hard too; he had to try to do and say the right things, but there was so much pressure. I loved him a lot, and this wasn't fair on anyone. I tried to think of myself when this had all happened; I was so small, so fragile – how could anyone do those things to a child? What kind of monster would hurt a child? I needed to recognise this, feel this, remember it, so that I could eliminate my own guilt and shame, the misguided feelings I had about feeling sorry for him that were still popping up in my brain. My thoughts were so mixed up – I just wanted to scream, *someone please help me*.

It's a strange feeling to recognise that you're falling apart, but also to be so frustrated at yourself. If anyone else had been going through this, I would have supported them 100 per cent, told them they were perfectly right to feel whatever way they felt, that all their emotions were the right emotions for them – but, because it was me, I was much harder on myself. I wanted to be a warrior, I wanted to be coping brilliantly, and I couldn't see that I was. Not at that point. Even when Vicky or any of the other support team members told me I was doing well, the doubt crept in. I heard Mum laughing at me, telling everyone I was stupid, dilatory, and it had more effect on me than any of the good or supportive comments.

When Dad, on 11 May, finally pleaded not guilty on all twenty-four counts, I was completely floored. I had known he probably would, but I guess a part of me had hoped he would have the decency to not put me through a trial. How wrong I was. All my emotions came out and the worry of the morning and this phone call left me in floods of tears. I was kind of glad I was alone. I didn't know how I would get through the next month, as he was clearly going to make me fight him. Would I have the strength? I felt numb and spent most of the day lying on my bed, losing time. He knew he did this and what he put me through, he knew he raped me, he knew what horrors I suffered – he took so much . . . but, suddenly, a light went on in my head. If I gave up, he would take the next forty years away from me too. I couldn't let him win and destroy my whole life, but God, I didn't want to have to fight in court. He had taken so much from me and he obviously didn't care; if he did, he would have accepted what he had done and admitted it.

The week that followed was one of my darkest ever. Elroy booked me a few days away – he felt I needed a break from my life to try to think more clearly and find the strength and anger that I needed to access in order to get through. Mum kept telling everyone she was going through so much and I felt she was looking forward to her day in court. She never once asked me how I was, how I was coping – but why would she? She had never been interested at any point in my life.

I was also reminded during this period, by an old school friend, Anna, that when we were thirteen, my dad pulled her shirt apart and said, 'Let's have a look.' She said I pushed his hands off her, shouting, 'Leave her alone', but I'd blocked this out. Anna said I also told her about the lock on the door. I still had so much guilt and shame – I hoped this trip Elroy had planned would help me.

It's exhausting to fight your own demons every day, Jenny, and I guess you knew that more than anyone. You wake up, and for that brief second before reality hits you, there is a freshness to the day. There is hope. Then, you remember who you are, what you have been through and how much fighting lies ahead. There are so many people who face this, face these challenges, and I think we all have those moments when we think, 'No, I can't do this any more.' But you can. You always can, because up until this point you have a track record of *always* having managed it. Be brave. Keep going. We've all been doing it for so long, with our scars, with our broken hearts. They will mend one day, in a different

186

way, but it will happen – we just need to keep going, keep pushing through, keep hoping that the light will shine and good people will win. If we don't believe that, then what is there? Our scars make us who we are; let's wear them proudly and throw this shame aside because it was never ours to bear, Jenny.

CHAPTER 9

FINDING MY STRENGTH
2011

I needed a break from everything really. I would have been happy to head off to a caravan but Elroy said I needed to escape properly, not be surrounded by things I recognised, so he booked me on a flight to Spain for five days in the hope that I could find some sort of strength that would get me through the trial. I left my phone behind and disappeared. I had been on my own in one sense for many parts of my life but, in a remote Spanish village, I had never felt so far away from other people. Cutting myself off was absolutely the right thing to do. Even on the flight over, I couldn't help but think that the only time I ever got to process things was when I was in bed – which tended to lead to a fitful, nightmare-filled sleep, and to greeting the morning feeling more tired than when I had gone to bed the night before.

No one was able to contact me or demand anything from me. It was a funny feeling and, to begin with, I was scared. I went to my hotel room, wondering what to do, worrying about whether Karl was all right without me. Thoughts were still running wild in my head and they were the same thoughts I had at home. I kept going back over experiences, trying to look clearly at things, attempting to work out when I could have stopped the bad stuff, when I could have chosen a different path – because, ultimately, I have always blamed myself. As the usual negative thinking washed over me, I was aware of something else – I felt as if the image of a little girl was there too, the child version of me, and I could see so clearly that she had no love and no affection apart from the twisted form of it that came from her father.

I spent four hours feeling battered, the negative voices in my head pushing me back to the image of that poor, emotionally starved child who needed me to be strong for her, but when I finally left my room, I did have a sense that I could now look at things from a healthier perspective. I always felt free in Spain – when Elroy and I had last lived there, the distance from my family helped a lot, and it still does. I had felt contentment back then and it started to come back quite quickly on this trip too. I knew this trip was needed to help me see through the fog.

I needed to grow stronger or I feared I wouldn't be able to get through the court case. Physically, I was already getting weaker – I had developed alopecia and lost a lot of weight – and emotionally, I was in bits, feeling weak and scared all of the time.

After wandering around for a while, I went back to my room and prepared for another night of restlessness; but to my surprise, I woke ten hours later having had the best night's sleep I could remember in years. It was a beautiful, sunny day and I spent a lot of it on the beach. A calmness always comes over me when I'm near the sea and I felt that I could start to think about things more clearly. Instead of thinking about my father, which was what I had expected to happen, it was Mum who came to my mind. I had often wondered to what extent she had known of the abuse, even whether she had colluded in it, and, on this day, flashes of too many things were coming into my head. Did she know what he was doing the whole time? I knew it would sound ludicrous to many people to even suggest that a mother could know of that kind of abuse of her child. But, after all, this was a woman who had never once hugged me, never willingly spent any time with me, never sang to me or told me stories or played with me. To her I was just an ugly, stupid, dilatory bitch.

I spent the whole of that second day thinking about Mum and it did me no good. I slept badly that night, and even the heat and sunshine of the following day didn't lift me from the terrible darkness that descended. I sat on the balcony and watched a man on the beach. He was carrying a little girl on his shoulders, and they were both laughing as he splashed in the sea. It was all innocent – but, to me, it was never that straightforward. Was he overstepping the mark? Should he be carrying her like that? What were his intentions? This was a battle that raged in my head so many times. I just automatically distrusted people, especially men, especially men when they were around children.

For me, attention from a father was only negative. When I didn't have it, I felt unloved and unwanted; when I did have it, I felt twisted and sick. To see a father have fun with his child, to love her naturally, was so alien to me that I couldn't process it normally. I saw threats where none existed; which was ironic, given that the people in my childhood had seen nothing where plenty existed.

That day, I was back to square one. I had felt some progress the day before, but now, all I could hear were the years of threats, the years of excuses, the constant stream of the same words he used to groom me and keep me in line. It was as if Dad was with me that day – his favourite phrases were ringing in my ears:

You're my princess.
I love you.
You're my queen.
If you were chocolate, I'd eat you.

I loved you more than anybody.

All dads and daughters do this.

It's normal, it's right.

Your mum's sick.

Do you want to break your mum's heart?

Your mum's too poorly for me to do these things with her.

Isn't it better for me to do these things with you than go to another woman and break up the family?

It's only skin.

It's no different to touching your arm or your leg.

There's nothing for you to worry about, because I can't get you pregnant.

I've had a vasectomy so there's nothing to be bothered with in that department.

You're not a virgin now and no one will think you are.

You have to do this to be ready for boys.

If your mum found out, it would kill her.

I have to do this – I'm a man, men need this.

If you don't do this, I'll be forced to cheat on your mum and it will kill her.

From my suitcase, I pulled out a book I had brought with me – one that I had thought would help me make sense of a few things. It was the memoir of someone who had been abused as a child too. The abuser in this case had also been the father, and the mother had been psychologically damaging just like mine, but I thought the similarities ended there. The reason I thought this was that, to me, there was one huge difference, a difference that, the more I read, the more I realised didn't exist. Until that point, until I read what that other woman went through, I had never thought of my dad as a paedophile. Everything fell away as the realisation hit. He had wanted a vulnerable child for his own sexual perversions – it was all about what he thought he was entitled to, and he was no different from all the others who had believed they could do this and get away with it. He was a monster who had preyed on an innocent little girl. When it started, I didn't know it was wrong; I trusted him and I had no one else to turn to. The fact that he had left when I turned sixteen showed me that he had no interest in me as an adult – it was the child who excited him, who made him feel powerful.

This was the truth and I was forty before it hit me. It had simply never occurred to me that he was a paedophile. I didn't put a label on it, or give it a name, until I read that book; it was just something that had happened. As I read that poor child's story, I recognised so much of it, but there was no denying what her father was. Finally, it all fell into place: that's what *my* dad was too.

My dad was a paedophile.

I said it in my head over and over again, then, choking

back the tears and the anger, I said it aloud, my voice getting louder and louder as I sat in my room.

'He was a paedophile, he was a paedophile, he was a paedophile!'

I finally felt the fury that I should have felt a long time ago. I thought about the times I had done the toilet in a plastic tub so he wouldn't get me if I went to the loo.

I thought about the times I had got into trouble for avoiding going upstairs to do my chores, and seeing him smirk at me as I left the room, knowing he would follow.

I thought about discovering the peepholes he had made in my door, and how I covered them, fearing I would be the one who was punished for that while he got away with his actions.

I thought about working out exactly which pieces of furniture fitted from the bed to the door to barricade it shut.

I was sure that he didn't care in the slightest about the fact that he had taken my life away. I was just there to be used for his gratification, and he seemed to have no conscience about what he did at all. The anger and the memories combined and I finally felt empowered. I wanted to keep that feeling but had no idea how I could make that happen. I wanted to face my anger, and this made me wonder whether I could even face him in court – could I do it without screens? Could I look him in the eye as I gave my testimony, force him to listen and see me as I described the lies, the terror, the existence of the child who had lived her life as it was a military operation? I had no idea, but the very fact that I was considering it was completely out of character.

I splashed my face with cold water and wandered out. My head was buzzing with all of these thoughts and the realisation of what my father was. Suddenly, I felt dizzy and knew I needed to sit down before I fainted. I couldn't remember eating anything that day, so I entered a café and ordered some food. I don't know how much time passed – I just kept asking for more coffee so that I could sit there. A few people asked me if I was all right but they were all men, so I just nodded and tried to not attract any attention. After a little while longer, one man in his sixties pulled up a chair and sat beside me. He was English, as were most of the tourists there, and he started talking, chatting away although I was keeping as quiet as I could. I nodded every so often but I just wanted him to leave me alone.

'If you're here tomorrow, why don't I take you somewhere nice?' the man said to me.

I just stared at him.

The empowered feelings from earlier had all gone and I realised that I actually didn't know how to say no. I had struggled with this all my life, not just in sexual situations, but when anyone asked me to do anything. I sometimes managed, but it was hard and I always felt wrong, a bad person, for turning any request down.

'So . . .' the man continued. 'Will you be here tomorrow? Are you up for it?'

Up for *what*? Even if he had been offering something as innocent as a walk, or another coffee, I would still have felt this panic that was rising in me. Dad had instilled in me a belief that a man has a right to sex, and I assumed that was what was being asked of me here. He made me believe that sex was essential to men and that there were always bad consequences when a man didn't get what he wanted in that department. It was ironic that I did feel this way given that, for me, as a child, the consequences were just as awful when he did get what he wanted.

With the very few partners I'd had, there had always been a struggle if I wanted to refuse them. I thought it was wrong of me. I thought they had a right to my body. I knew I only valued myself as a physical being, and that was a low value anyway. What was inside was rotten and if people got too close, they would hate me once they saw what I truly was. There was, in my mind, nothing to like.

That man in the café must have thought I was mad. I truly don't know whether he was propositioning me or not, because my mind started racing and my body was flooded with panic. I mumbled some excuse, threw money on the table and ran out, rushing back to my room. For the rest of that day and night, I beat myself up terribly. How could I have been so deluded as to think that I had any power? How could I have thought I might be able to face Dad in court?

Over the next day, my mind was filled by thoughts of the power of my dad's conditioning. I don't think he believed I would ever tell – maybe he just assumed he would be able to forget about it, write it off as something that happened a long time ago. It's not like that for survivors; we can't write it off or forget it. If he had any conscience, he wouldn't have been putting me through the trial, he would have admitted everything. I was disgusted with myself in so many ways – and my behaviour in the café the day before hadn't helped matters – but there was a little voice there saying, *You have changed; you did report him, you did want him to be punished and that takes strength.* Why was the time right now, I wondered?

I don't think to begin with that it was about making him accountable to me; I think it was all about whether he had access to any other children. It was only when someone else – Vicky – had said he needed to pay that I had even thought it could be done. I didn't want to be scared for the rest of my life. Both of my parents stripped me bare; they took away my confidence, self-respect and even my body. They made me believe I was nothing, that I wasn't worthy of anyone's love, and I still thought that most of the time.

I couldn't bear to leave my room that day, but that

night I wandered out to watch the sunset and hugged myself tightly. I was going back home to something I couldn't even imagine. I'd never been in a court before, never given evidence, and I was paralysed with fear every time I thought of it. It was as if my head was full of the people saying, *You can't do this, you won't win, historical abuse is almost impossible to prove, everyone will see you for the dirty little girl you are.* I knew all of that; I knew it too well. The chances of securing a conviction were minuscule; but I owed it to myself and to any other children who might be protected if Dad was revealed as what he was.

The following morning, I packed my bags and walked outside to sit down on a little stone bench to wait for the taxi to pick me up for the airport. I thought of Karen, the baby, the little girl, the teenager. All of those versions of me, all with the same scared, lost look. I mentally hugged her and made a commitment to who I had been and who I hoped to be. I told the child within me that she deserved to be free of all of this, that she was a good soul who should have a happy, peaceful life. I mentally held her hand and thought of Jenny. I wanted to make my dad accountable for what he had done.

There's only me – the little girl has gone. Jenny has gone. He made his choices – I had no choice then but I do now. I need the strength to do this; it matters more than anything.

I finally cried. I cried for that little girl who'd had so much taken away from her, and for my sister.

I got back after five days of being completely alone, no phone, no family, no problems or stress, nothing. Just me, to think and try to find strength. My mind must have been crying out for this, because I started to feel better immediately. The minute the plane took off my mind started to think, go back, accept, make sense. I tried to hold on to what I had achieved during the trip. I remembered that, by day three, I had almost sorted my mind out and, for the first time, it had occurred to me – he's a paedophile who used his own little girl for his sexual pleasure; he had never loved or cared for me and never been remorseful. He'd had twenty-five years to apologise to me and he surely wouldn't put me through this if he genuinely felt guilt.

By day five, I had felt ready. I no longer wanted screens in court – why should I hide away? I wanted to look at him. I wanted him to know I was no longer afraid and I wanted to look at him when he gave his evidence. I shouldn't have to hide behind a screen and then scurry away like the frightened little girl I used to be. I needed to face this, face him and hopefully move forward with my life. I came home feeling good – the confusion had gone and so had my shame (I hoped). I needed to hold on to this strength for three more weeks. I hoped I could. He wasn't sorry; he wasn't remorseful – he used a vulnerable child, took forty years from me and left a scared shell of a woman: but no more. It had to change now. I deserved that.

As we moved into June, I still felt strong. My trip had been so important and needed – and Elroy had done absolutely the right thing in encouraging me to go. I needed all the strength I could muster, as I found out in this period that Kev did not want to give evidence; he said he didn't need the hassle and wanted a quiet life. I wasn't sure if he could choose – can they make him give evidence, I wondered? I guessed the main thing was that, yet again, he had hurt me deeply. He hadn't been there for me, just like when he supported Dad over me, and when he retracted his claim that he too had been abused.

I tried to stay positive, but it was starting to slip. I was falling back into fear and I didn't want that to happen; I wanted to be strong again, I wanted to be that warrior. A court visit was planned for me so that I could see where everything would be and where things would happen. I really hoped this would help because I was starting to feel very wobbly, and I kept arguing with Elroy because the stress was so bad. I don't think people on the outside realise that, when you start this whole process, you're signing up to a sentence yourself as well as committing your loved ones to it. There was barely a moment when I didn't think about what lay ahead – even when my head didn't actively acknowledge it, my body did. My stomach churned, my head pounded – I wonder if the abusers, the rapists and the paedophiles feel the same? I would guess many of them don't – they probably feel aggrieved, they probably think only of themselves as they always have.

I think one of the reasons I have always wanted to document my whole journey is to show it warts and all, to show people that it isn't a matter of just making the decision 'to tell' and then the court case with verdict happens. Life is in all the minutes that take place before and after that, the middle of the night when you wake up sweating and shaking from night terrors, the flashbacks that happen when you're in the supermarket, the horror that hits you when you've been singing along to the car radio seconds before. It isn't cut and dried, it isn't black and white; it's a mess of emotion, a mess of the past and present and future with no clear exit strategy.

I was surprised by how small the court seemed to be – but it still had a huge effect on me. My grand heroic gesture of 'I don't need screens' went out the window as soon as I saw it, and as soon as I saw how close Dad would be to me. He would only be sitting about twenty feet away. I couldn't stop shaking and kept looking at the seat he would be in. I thought I would need the security of the screens after all. I also found out that I would be questioned by both sides, but only on my statement, no one else's – they said I could see it any time to refresh my memory. I didn't need to. I knew it and I didn't need to look at it again. It was the truth and it wouldn't change –

as long as I stuck to the facts, I'd be true to myself and no one could trip me up on anything.

After the court visit, the nightmares wouldn't stop. I kept dreaming that Dad had me trapped and all of the horrible stuff, all of the abuse, replayed time after time. Vicky supported me as ever, but the nights were mine and I had to battle those alone. In houses everywhere, in the dead of night, there are women, men, children, who will face their tormentors the next day or week or month, and we all dread when darkness comes and we know the faces will return to us from our past.

I thought I would try to get away for a few days again to get my strength back, as that had worked last time. I wanted this to change my life. I wanted to fight for the little Karen, the tiny girl who broke my heart. I wanted to give her a big hug and make it all OK. I wanted a real life, to feel normal, to be normal for my son – everyone deserved it; they deserved a strong me. So I did – I went away for a few days; but when I got back from the airport the day before the trial was due to start, Elroy sat me down.

'He's admitted it,' he told me. 'Well, he's admitted some of it.'

I felt a wave of mixed emotions – anger that it was only 'some', but relief that he had admitted anything. The judge had asked the liaison team to come and tell me in person and I found out from them that he had admitted ten of the twenty-four counts. They were not what I had hoped for, to be honest. They were 'only' the ones relating to when I was over the age of eleven, and they were 'indecent assault' rather than sexual assault, things such as touching my chest. Tina and Tamsin from the liaison support group told me that, if I accepted this, if I agreed that he would be found guilty on these charges alone, it would be over.

'Over?' I whispered. 'What do you mean? It will never be over, not if he doesn't have to face up to it.'

'You don't have to decide right now,' they told me. 'The decision doesn't have to be made until tomorrow – we all hope you find the strength to do this though, Karen. Us, the judge, the police team, the CPS . . . we're all with you.'

Nodding, I let them out – I did want to fight it, I did want to be strong enough to say, no, it isn't enough to say you 'touched my chest' when I was eleven; but I wanted to spare everyone so much that I just accepted it. I'd go with what he was willing to admit, and let him call the shots again.

But what about me, Jenny? What about us? If I just say 'Fine!', he'll get a slap on the wrist and everyone will just think I made a fuss about nothing. In fact, they'll probably think he didn't even do the things he is willing to admit to. They'll probably think he's the good man again. That he is admitting to things he didn't do just out of some fatherly duty, to stop the mad daughter having to go through it all. That's what they always thought, isn't it? That Norman Yeo was a saint – that he took on Mum and her bastards, took them on as his own, and only had his fishing trips as an escape from it all. But we had no escape, did we? No escape from him or for her. If I let him get away with this, if I don't even try to fight for us, where does that leave your legacy? I want the world to remember you, Jenny, and this is a part of me trying to achieve that. I want to tell your story, and I can't be true to that story if I don't stand up in court and say what he did to me.

So, I made up my mind to do it. I decided that the vague notion of a 'possible' maximum two-year sentence if his plea was accepted just wasn't enough. There was also the chance that he would get no sentence at all, even having accepted those few charges. I needed closure. I actually felt quite shocked at what he was proposing, and the anger started to build and I knew in my heart that I needed to go ahead with the trial. I thought a lot about my sister that night. I couldn't sleep, again, and got up at 1.30am to go to the loo. The moon was shining straight into my bed when I got back into it, right through my window, although the sky was cloudy. It might sound crazy but I felt like it was a sign from Jenny. I told her, *I will do good*

*for us both, for what we went through. I'll manage this –
but I'll need you there beside me.*

On the day I needed to give evidence – Tuesday, 22
June 2011, a date I will never forget – I was shattered. I
had been up all night. We both had; Elroy had paced the
floor with me. I felt scared of what the following hours
would bring but I also had a feeling that my whole life has
been about this day. We were collected at 8.30am by Tina
and Tamsin and made our way to court.

Here we go, I thought to myself.

We headed in through the witness entrance and into
the suite allocated for me. Here I met the barrister, Mr
McNally, for the first time. I think it might surprise a lot
of people to hear that you don't meet your barrister until
that point; there was certainly no previous relationship,
although I guess he had spent a lot of time on my files
and statements. He was nice, friendly, and he put me at
ease. He went through my statement and told me the
things he didn't want me to answer – I was to avoid
hearsay, mostly. This turned out to be good advice and
I'm glad he told me. I had to wait in the witness suite.
My head was spinning. Tamsin and Tina were with me,
and Melanie and Ian, but I decided to go into the suite
on my own. I thought I'd be stronger that way but when
Melanie asked at the last minute if I wanted her to come
in, I agreed. In the end, I was glad of a face I knew when
it got tough.

Two hours after arriving, the court usher turned up to take me into court.

'Don't worry,' she said, smiling. 'It'll all be over soon.'

I wondered if that was true. Was this the start of it ending, or just another horrible chapter? I was amazed at how terrified I felt. I was also still in shock that Dad had even turned up, as over the past few months I'd feared so much that he would harm himself and not come to court at all. But there he was; he had tried to admit those few minor charges, which hadn't worked, so it was crystal clear that he was going to make me fight all the way. Actually, I told myself, it was a good thing that my misguided feelings about him having any remorse or being sorry were slowly but surely being completely squashed. I also found out that morning that Kevin knew he must attend court, that he had no choice – but he said he would turn up only so he wouldn't be sent to prison for non-attendance, and that he was intending to refuse to talk on the stand.

Just before I went in, I was told the defence barrister had accepted my brothers' statements as fact, which meant they didn't have to be cross-examined; their statements would be read out in court instead. In those statements, Ian and Andrew said they wanted to help; they felt they didn't do anything as kids and they wanted to help now. This made me very sad. Just giving a statement is a massive help and great support. It wasn't their job to help me when we were children. It wasn't their job to be my protector. It was our parents' job and they failed us, both of them.

When I entered court, my legs felt as though they didn't have the strength to hold me. I felt hot and dizzy and overwhelmed. The curtain was already pulled over and the judge and the jury were absent. The usher took me through the little half door and down two steps into the witness box, located next to the judge. The jury box was directly in front of me and the barristers were to my right. Because of the screen, my barrister was behind Dad instead of to his right, and I knew Dad was there.

He's there.

Jenny, he's there.

CHAPTER 10

THE TRIAL

I just sense him, I just sense his very presence as if it's oozing out towards me.

His barrister is a craggy-looking man who constantly stares at me over the top of his glasses. I feel intimidated by this but maybe that's his plan. I'm later told that Dad looks about a hundred years old, and his face seems to have collapsed. I don't want to feel one jot of sympathy for him, but I wonder what the reaction of the jury will be to this pathetic, pitiful creature. I want them to see him as he was; I want them to see the man who raped me over thirty years ago, not this weary, bewildered pensioner.

The jury is brought in while the usher gives me tissues and water. I watch them out of the corner of my eye. I think the jury is made up of eight women and four men, but I'm not 100 per cent sure. My barrister smiles at me and I think I might fall over purely out of feeling so overwhelmed. The presence of him, of my dad, feels enormous to me.

For an hour, maybe an hour and a half, my barrister gently talks me through my statement. It is more difficult than I could ever have imagined. He constantly pushes me on issues, pushing for more details, pushing, pushing, pushing, and I want to stop, I want to not have to say the words – but I know I must do this. He must do this for the sake of the jury. I knew this would be hard, but I find it so difficult to actually 'say' the things that happened. I am aware that my father is sitting twenty feet away from me, listening, as it goes on. I try to concentrate on the questions and make myself less aware of his presence, but it's hard to actively ignore something when it seems to loom so large. I look either at my barrister or above the jurors. The questions are very, very sensitive and some of the answers I have to give do make me cry. The details are very personal and I feel ashamed saying them.

Relief floods through me when it's over. I've noticed some of the jury trying to make eye contact with me, but I try to avoid it as I don't know if it's allowed. The judge is stony-faced. I can't guess what he's thinking. After my barrister has finished, the judge asks me if I am OK to carry on. I'm dreading this bit even more but I say 'Yes' and the barristers switch places.

The first angle Dad's barrister tries is that I am confused. He says that I think I can remember but I am mistaken. He says I'm bewildered about ages and houses and other 'facts'. I tell him I'm not. I do feel intimidated by how he looks at me and how he talks to me – and, at first, the intimidation works. I'm shaking like a leaf and keep asking myself, where is my strength, when is it going to come? This man is calm, collected, educated; he knows the system inside and out, and he's trying to trip me up on little things so that the big things shatter too. I know what he's trying to do – if I can't remember what age I was, or what house I lived in, how can I be trusted with allegations that could ruin a man's life? But I do know. I do remember. I tell myself, *remember you are only telling the truth; you can't be tripped up on the truth, just state the facts.* One of the legal team had said to me, 'If you knew everything on a timeline, you wouldn't be believed by the jury. You can't know the dates of everything, you can't know the detail of everything – stick to what you *do* know, stick to the truth and don't embellish it.'

It's very harsh though. I feel nauseous and shaky. In my hand is a small crystal that Jenny gave me years ago, and I turn it round and round as the barrister goes over and over the same points. In my mind, I keep saying to her, *This is for us, Sis. This is for all the hurt against us both.* Jenny can't take the stand and say what happened, and little Karen is now gone. I'm the only one left. It is up to me to tell the truth.

Surprisingly, the more the barrister accuses me – calls me a liar, says I am exaggerating, says I've made things up – the stronger I feel. I'm not weak. I'm really not. I just insist that I am telling the truth, and I do remember what happened. I believe Jenny sent me strength that day and the more he tries to undermine me, the more she makes me feel that I can do this.

At 1pm, it's time for the first break. I go to meet Vicky, who says I am doing fine, and Ian and Elroy. I can't eat anything. I walk back to court with Vicky. I hear my dad mumbling to someone as we go back in and I try to walk with my eyes closed as we go past him.

The afternoon cross-examination takes forever and it feels like Dad's barrister goes over the same points again and again – what school, what house? It was harder to go back into court in the afternoon, probably because I knew what I was facing.

Even as I am writing this, I am still feeling the shock. How did I do it? Where did I find the strength? How did I finally manage to stand up for myself? Dad did do those things to me, he did take away my life for so long, he did leave me damaged; please, please let this be a new start for me, I pray inwardly. Please let me be able to build on what I'm managing here.

The questions go on and on and on. At one point, I look

at the little door/hatch thing at the side and imagine myself just running through it. I feel at times that I can't take any more – how much longer will he keep questioning me, and how much longer will my strength hold? His questions again and again and again. He is ruthless and calls me a liar, says I made things up. He says personal things and, at times, I feel light-headed. I don't know how my legs are holding me up. I keep turning Jenny's crystal over in my hand and, eventually, I develop a coping strategy – I just take it one question at a time. Don't think backwards, Karen, don't think forwards, I tell myself; one question at a time. This seems to help.

At 3.45pm, the judge turns into my saviour.

'Do you have much more to ask?' he enquires.

'Not really,' replies the barrister.

'This is going to be over today,' says the judge, and my heart leaps. 'Get on with it.'

I think he figured the same as me; I suspected that the barrister was trying to get his questioning to roll over to the next day. He has kept flicking through his papers and scrolling through his laptop, as if he was trying to find more questions, because I disputed every lie or accusation he threw at me.

The thought of it rolling over terrified me. I genuinely thought it was a possibility until the judge stepped in, and I did think to myself, *I can't come back here tomorrow, not when he has had a whole night to figure out more accusations and questions, and to find more stuff to throw at me.* I don't know what I would have done if it had happened, so thank goodness for the judge. Court usually ends at about 4pm but, just before then, the barrister finds what he thinks is a discrepancy in my statement. The judge sends me out to read through it and I immediately find what he's going on about.

He keeps picking out differences between my statement and my personal notes. I say eight or nine times that these notes were personal memories that were only ever for me, for my eyes, when I had sat and tried to make sense of what was in my head; putting it on paper helped but they were only ever for me, they weren't for a forensic examination. I was upset when the police took them away and one of the most devastating things about the whole trial is this point, when I realise everybody in that court has a copy of my personal thoughts, my horrible memories and my private words that I never wanted anyone else to ever see. This is very hard to deal with. Now the barrister is trying to pick holes in all of it – but he can't, because I'm sticking to my rule: only tell the truth.

* * *

Court finally finished just after 5pm and I remember the judge looking at me and nodding kindly as I said, 'Can I go now?' I nearly stumbled up the two steps as I left the witness box. I don't think I have ever felt so out of control of my own body. I kept thinking, *they'll call me back*. I didn't think it was really done with. The thought haunted me as I sobbed outside that courthouse. My barrister told me I had done well and wished me good luck. Everyone said I was brave and strong, but it certainly didn't feel that way. I tried to rush everyone away as I knew Dad would be out soon – he was to go and sign the Sex Offenders Register as he had already admitted some charges, but then he was free to leave, as nothing had been decided yet. He was still a free man.

* * *

The evening goes by in a blur. I am in shock, scared, relieved, proud, sad, all rolled into one. I also can't get Jenny out of my mind. I'm not a religious person but I wonder if she's looking down on me and if she's feeling proud. I couldn't have done this without the memory of her and her crystal, but I know we still have a long way to go.

* * *

The next day in court, the biggest thing is Mum's evidence. It only takes a couple of hours for that and her cross-examination. I am obviously not there, but I am told later by people who were that there are a lot of contradictions. She does admit a few things though, and I hope they show that I was telling the truth. She says she put a lock on my bedroom door when she caught him in there, again when I was thirteen, and that she also found him going through my underwear.

Some parts of the evidence only bring up her side, but I guess that's always the case in court. When she admits Dad had put me in their bed, she says her back was to me, and she snapped at him, 'What did you bring her in here for?' Mum tells the court that she allowed me to stay in the bed when he did that to keep me safe; I can't challenge that, but can only hope the jurors see that it never achieved that aim, even if that's what she was trying to do, and that putting me back in my own locked room, and getting rid of the man she kept finding with me, would have been a much better option.

Mum is asked by my barrister what her relationship with me was like, and she said it was hit and miss but most of the time we had got on.

Maybe that's what she thought. Maybe she did actually feel that, most of the time, we got on. What I remember, though, is that she continually discussed her sex life with me from when I was tiny, she told me about abuse, she told me about rape, she said she had sticks pushed into her, that she was forced to have sex with another woman. Who am I to say what was true and what wasn't? I can only repeat what I was told. But, combining all of that with other things she said and how she acted, I am wary of believing any single word.

I am covered in scars – my buttocks, my private area; a triangular one at the back of my knee and I have one from a cut on the side of my eye – but none of these injuries were ever treated by medics. How does that fit with looking after your child, and keeping them safe?

When the barrister asks if she knew what was going on about the lock, Mum just says it was to keep my dad out. She tells the barrister that she asked me what was going on, and I said 'Nothing', so she believed me.

I am told that Mum looked at Dad constantly as she said these things, and that there were smirks from her side, but I wasn't there and I can't prove it; all I know is that although she told the jury I confided in her, surely they would have realised from my evidence that this would never have happened? The very notion of confiding in or trusting my mother was the opposite of every part of our relationship. My emotions are everywhere – I'm relieved to not be called back, worried I still might be, worried my mother will have made the jury doubt me; I just feel drained.

In his statement, Andy says he saw Dad coming out of my bedroom naked and going into the bathroom, then going back in. He mentioned the food we had to eat back then and mapped out the house and address perfectly, and it all tallies with what I have said. He had seen Dad coming out of my bedroom with an erection when he was ten – he had carried that all his life. His statement, and Kev's, are read out the afternoon after Mum gives her evidence, but they aren't cross-examined. They are just accepted.

* * *

When morning breaks on the Thursday, I'm barely standing. Today is the day that Dad will give his evidence. Elroy and Ian will sit in, and they will tell me everything. It's only scheduled to last a couple of hours. I was on the stand for much longer, which seems ridiculous. He still insists he only started after I was eleven and that it was very 'minor' touching.

* * *

Apparently, Dad admitted that he had been attracted to me in 'that way', and stood with his head down a lot. Elroy told me the jury were looking at him with what seemed like disgust, as was the court clerk and sometimes even the judge, but I wondered if he was just saying this to make me feel better. At one point, the judge ordered a ten-minute recess and said he needed some time in a dark room; that he couldn't possibly go on. I had hoped the judge and jury weren't buying Dad's lies for one moment, and this action from the judge gave me a little hope as it made me feel that he was seeing how awful it all was.

At one point there was a legal argument over consent, my age and a change in a 2003 law, so the jury was sent out while it was discussed. At another point, Ian lost it and stood up and said, 'How could she consent, she was a child?' He got told off by the judge, but I was so proud of him for saying that.

* * *

'I think it changed, though,' Elroy tells me later that day, 'when they started to put things to him towards the end of the morning and he admitted they were possible. Surely they'll see that this means he's guilty?'

'I don't know, I really don't know,' I tell him. 'I have no idea which way this will go. I keep telling myself it wouldn't have got this far if there wasn't a chance they would believe me.'

'It'll all work out,' Elroy says. 'There's nothing you can do now – we just have to wait.'

Dad's questioning continues after lunch and, at the end of the day, I meet up with Elroy, Ian and Andy. I take Ian to the side and he starts to cry, saying he's sorry, that he didn't know, that he feels guilty, that he can't handle the things he's heard. I try to reassure him that it was not his responsibility to protect me – it was theirs and they didn't do it. I tell him the guilt was theirs too, not mine, not his. We think the jury will go home tomorrow – will it be hours, or days, until they come back?

Elroy tells me that when they left court they bumped into Dad, literally. Elroy dragged Ian away and says he started sobbing like a little boy, uncontrollably. He really wasn't prepared to face a man with whom he had demons of his own. Ian says, 'It was his voice, his voice took me back.' It has been so hard for him to hear the details of what happened. I am heartbroken for my big brother when Elroy tells me all this, but there is also a part of me that's scared of how Elroy himself might see me, now he knows what had actually gone on. I never wanted anyone to know the details, especially anyone close to me, and here I am with my partner and older brother, knowing that they knew. This is so difficult for me; I feel such shame and embarrassment.

***

On the Friday, Elroy and Ian go to court for the judge's summing-up. It takes about two hours and Elroy feels that the judge is leaning towards my side. Bless him – he would say that, I guess, as he's so protective and supportive; I can't let myself feel any hope yet.

The jury is sent out at 12.30pm and everyone hangs around the court except for me and my friend Nicky, who wait in a cafe. I had known Nicky for twelve years by this time. She was a complete rock for me; she came to court each time or sat in the cafe with me while I took some time to find strength. We are still very close and I'll never forget how much she did for me during this time.

My head is all over the place. I convince myself that he will be found not guilty, that I haven't been believed.

I guess the demons are still with me and my fear of being seen as a liar has never gone away. I feel dizzy and nauseous and can't think or talk straight. Around 2.30pm, I am discussing with Nicky whether I should go and hear the verdict when Elroy calls her and says, 'Stay there.'

This is it.

I honestly don't know which way it will go, but I feel a physical reaction to the fact that it's been decided. I get up and go outside, only to see them all walking down the street towards me. For some reason, my mother is there too.

Elroy rushes up to me, takes my arm and says, 'Less than two hours, Karen.'

My heart falls and I think I will pass out.

Then he says, 'Guilty, Karen, every single count, every single juror, clean sweep.'

I can't take it in. He's saying my father was found guilty on every count, unanimously? I feel numb. I believe I was in complete shock. Everyone is happy but I can't feel anything; they all hug me but I don't know how to react. As my mother approaches, I just say, 'No – stay away from me!'

I gradually come back to some sort of awareness while Elroy holds me close. I hear that Dad has been bailed until 18 July to get his affairs in order – this is a shock, to be honest; I can't believe he's allowed to walk free for any time at all. A little voice inside me wonders if he will get away with it – what if they change their minds while he's out and about? I quickly realise I am being silly, and that this isn't how it works at all.

We all go back into the cafe for a cup of tea and I call Vicky – she cries on the phone and my first bit of emotion shows as I start to weep too, with relief, sadness, pent-up emotion. I'm not sure what I am feeling. Everyone is talking, saying they're happy, saying how well I did. But what did I do, really? I just said the truth, told everyone what had happened, spoke the words that were facts and didn't deviate from what had happened. I don't feel like celebrating; everyone is laughing and is relieved, but I feel as if I'm watching them rather than being a part of it.

Mum says she roared and applauded when the verdicts came in one by one, and thanked the jurors individually. She must have forgotten Elroy was sitting right beside her because I'll later find out this is a lie; she did none of those things but just sat quietly. She's in and out of the cafe, on her phone all the time – to whom? Karl gives me a big hug and everyone is chattering and laughing and texting people.

Half an hour later, I go outside to talk to Tamsin on the phone, and she's so happy at the result; she has put a lot of emotional time into this. She wanted to be there right up until the end but couldn't make the verdict today. She can't believe it took less than two hours to decide on all the remaining counts; she believes their minds were made up after I gave my evidence. As I'm talking to her on the street, I turn round and my dad is walking towards me. I can't believe it. He's dressed in black, pulling a large black suitcase, smoking a cigarette. I run into a doorway next to a shop, a big wooden door – and he walks straight past. I'm surprised that I don't really feel anything.

The day goes by in a haze of phone calls and even the next few weeks are a little blurry. Everyone wants to celebrate apart from me; I just feel sadness and a sense of loss for the life I should have had. I hear nothing from Kevin or my mother but I hear she's going around telling everyone all about it, playing up to her role as a victim and getting free drinks on the back of it all. Kevin is heartbroken that his dad is in prison and has decided he can't talk to me as I was the one who brought it about – I can understand his confusion but have to admit I am hurt by it. Andy is a different kettle of fish altogether, and says he's glad that he told his truth and that it helped. Elroy and I are stronger than ever; this has had only a positive effect on us, and the relief of it being over is showing in me now – I feel happier and closer to him than I have in years. We are starting to laugh again.

I decide I must go to the sentencing in order to get closure and to hear those most important words, 'You did this.' I am afraid of it, afraid of what I might feel and of seeing him again, but it's necessary. I've done harder things.

Monday 18 July 2011 is when it's scheduled to happen, at 10.30am. Gail arrives on the Sunday and I book her into a hotel across from court; I am so grateful to her for being there as she makes an incredibly tense day into one with a few surprising laughs. On the day itself, we're not sure where to go, so I head up to the court canteen with Gail, while Nicky and Elroy work out the logistics. They come back to tell me, but I'm horrified when I realise the walk to court will mean walking past Dad as he's sitting waiting. I have found this throughout the whole process – there simply isn't enough separation of complainant and accused. It's a dreadful situation and one that could be so easily remedied. It takes about half an hour to build up the courage to do it. When I do, and we get to the court vestibule area, we are just sent out. So we head down to witness care, which it turns out is where we should have gone in the first place! Vicky, Tina and Tamsin all come along – they want to see the outcome too and I am so grateful for their support. They have been absolute rocks throughout all of this.

We are told we could be waiting hours, but then we are suddenly called in. We have to go into the public gallery, where there are just enough seats for us all, plus a couple sitting on the end who I don't know. I sit between Gail and Nicky but wish I was sitting beside Elroy. The court is full of people, just as it was during the trial, but there is no jury now. My father is sitting directly in front of me with a guard. He's wearing a blue shirt and dark trousers, and doesn't look up much. He's wringing his hands and looks agitated. I feel as though my head will burst; I'm terrified. I'm shaking like a leaf and feel sick. I try to look everywhere except at him.

We stand for the judge.

I'm not at all prepared for what happens next: my barrister goes back over the whole case, details I had hoped I would never have to hear again. Nicky and Gail know none of this and it proves too much for me to hear such personal details read out in front of more people I love. I have to leave the court.

Vicky comes out to me. I am so, so upset. She calms me down and helps me get rid of the guilt I'm feeling about the situation. She says it's normal, as I'm a human being with real emotions and I am a good person, but that he needs to be stopped from hurting anyone else. This makes me feel better – she is truly an angel. I stay out until both barristers have finished talking, and go back in for the summary. I do hear what I need to hear – the judge tells him, 'You took away her childhood and ruined her life. You say you are disgusted in yourself and so you should be. She should have been kept safe in her own home. The lengths she went to, in order to keep away from you, make horrific evidence to hear.'

During the whole summing-up, the judge looks everywhere else, but not at him. Not even once. There are lots of different sentences handed down: one year, two years, four years, three; but the longest is sixteen years, of which he will have to serve eight before he can apply for parole. He is also put on the Sex Offenders Register for life and will never be able to live or work near children or vulnerable adults.

Then the judge says, 'Take him down.'

As my father stands up to be led away, he turns a little, and I think he's going to say something . . . but he doesn't.

I feel flushed; my head and face are burning. I'm completely shocked at the length of the sentence – sixteen years (everything else is concurrent). When we leave court, Tamsin says it's the longest sentence her department has known. Vicky says it's the longest she's ever heard of in all the time she's worked in this area. Yet again everyone is happy and wanting to celebrate, but I can't feel the same way; I never have. This has to be a new start for me, I think, and I hope that I'll feel some sort of release inside sometime soon.

I thank everyone, including the barrister, police, Vicky and the support team, then we walk into town.

'Is this it?' I ask Elroy. 'Is then when my life finally starts?'

'It is,' he tells me. 'If you want it, it is.'

I've felt it so easy to talk to you throughout all of this, Jenny, but I don't know what to say now. How odd is that? I was so glad he had been found guilty, that someone had finally called him to account, but I also wished that someone had been called to account for you. The dead have no voice. Their stories can be told by others, and I have tried to do that, but I wish the words could come directly from you and I wish you could be here to make sure your tormentors had to face up to what they did to you.

When I decided to tell our story, I thought I wouldn't have the strength to do it under my own name. I still felt shameful and I still felt dirty. I don't feel that way now – I feel that I can stand up, proud, and say, this is who I am. That day, I changed my name to 'Caryn' and I vowed I would never be called 'Yeo' again. I reclaimed myself. I also never called him 'Dad' again – he was just 'Norman'. The paedophile who had tried to break me. Just that, a man who had made his own choices and who now had to pay the price for those choices. I wasn't his daughter, and I wasn't ever going to be ashamed again. I would live for both of us, Jenny, I would tell the world that my big sister deserved to be remembered with every last breath in my body.

CHAPTER 11

SENTENCES
THEN UNTIL
NOW

An hour after we left court, Grandma's nursing home called to say she was really poorly, so Elroy and I went straight over there. For the next thirty-six hours I didn't leave her bedside but, sadly, she left us at 3am on the Wednesday morning. I was devastated, heartbroken at the loss of her but I also knew she was so tired of life and wanted to be with my grandpa, who had passed twenty-six years earlier. I felt that God works in mysterious ways – I was blessed that I got to spend her last hours with her, which I wouldn't have if Norman was around. I arranged her funeral and made all the plans for her. Norman had all of her documents in prison so I didn't know what would happen regarding them once he was informed of her death. Neither he nor Kev came to her funeral, but it was a lovely day for her, with songs I chose that I knew she would have loved. I was glad I was able to do this for her but I missed her so much already.

It was a strange time, but also one that brought some normality into my life. Everyone goes through this, losing elderly relatives – it's just natural, just normal, and it was something I could deal with. Even missing Grandma is part of life's cycle, and I hold on to my lovely memories of her. She was a wonderful woman who did not deserve to have anything nasty brought into her life. I'm glad she never knew about Norman's conviction and I genuinely felt he was the way he was because of his choices, not because of anything that he experienced at the hands of my grandparents. People have to take responsibility for who they are – and I never saw anything that suggested Grandma and Grandpa were anything other than loving people. They were horrified by the lazy, indolent life Mum and Norman lived, and he certainly hadn't been brought up that way, but even if he had, I don't think that's an excuse. I think it's a horrible slur to suggest that those who have been abused in any way can't prevent themselves from becoming abusers. There is nothing in this world that would make me hurt a child, and I hate the fact that some people believe you can never break the cycle of abuse. Grandma was a good woman, and I can only hope it's her blood that runs through my veins rather than his.

I was so relieved that Norman got such a long sentence, because it did matter, it really did. Knowing that all of those people – strangers who had no reason to do anything other than listen to the facts and make a decision based on those facts – believed me meant the world. However, I think the fact that we are so unused to substantial sentences being handed out to paedophiles, particularly with regards to historical cases of child abuse, is a sad indictment of our society.

Yes, Norman got sixteen years, but I got a life sentence.

When someone reveals that they are a survivor of child sexual abuse, the focus is on that specific crime and on the fact that they did survive it – but so much is hidden.

I've fought a battle with bulimia for sixteen years now. I am never free from guilt or shame.

I only had one child because I could barely cope with the anxiety and fear of raising a child in the world that had allowed my father to abuse me. I felt incredible anxiety and terror every time Karl was around other people and, for years, I thought I couldn't risk having another baby if that was to be how I felt. I wanted a little girl so badly, but I worried about how I would be, whether I could ever allow her to be around men. When I finally did feel strong enough, I found that I had been so physically damaged by the abuse that I would never have another, that Karl was actually a miracle child in so many ways.

I suffer from depression and have done for years; I have

suicidal thoughts and I really can't say with any certainty that I won't act on them one day. I get flashbacks and have nightmares, which haunt me during my waking hours too.

I don't really trust many people and I have ongoing issues with intimacy: seeing Norman's face when I'm with someone, knowing there are so many triggers that can ruin any moment no matter how much I'm loved by the other person.

I'm unable to be alone with older men and I think of every one of them as a potential paedophile. I look to see if they're hanging around children in a suspicious way; I check everywhere all the time just to see if I can 'spot' one, even though I know the danger is much more likely to lie closer to home, just as it did with me.

I always seek approval from other people, even when I know they aren't worth it. I feel worthless, and let others use me, expecting their hurt and just waiting for the moment it will come.

I've tried so hard to be honest in this book and cover everything, but I've really only scratched the surface – how do you put a life, all of those lives, into a couple of hundred pages?

To this day, my mother's voice is there in my mind far too often, shouting me down, telling me I'm stupid. I feel that there is a darkness on me that other people can see, that I have been marked for ever by the past, what was done to me. But I must find the strength to move on.

Many – if not most – abuse survivors are told that historical convictions are virtually impossible to achieve. That isn't surprising really: it's hard enough for contemporary cases to secure a 'guilty' verdict and, even when they do, custodial sentences are not guaranteed. With historical allegations, there is likely to be even less evidence, witnesses may be impossible to trace or have died and corroboration is difficult to prove. I knew all of this – I was told many times – but still I fought. And I won.

In the middle of all of this, Vicky has been amazing. She tells me she will offer support for as long as I need it. She says some cases stay with her always, and that mine is one of them. It's been in the local papers, so everyone knows now, but I'm handling that. I'm still waiting for my 'elation' to start, to start wanting to celebrate, but I kind of doubt that it will ever happen. I hope my life is better now though. I was believed; it was his fault, not mine. It's my turn to have a life now. For the first time he knows how it feels to be afraid and out of control of his own life. I awoke one night recently thinking, *I'm free and safe, no one is going to hurt me.* The tables had completely turned. In fact, after the trial, early one morning when I was driving to Birmingham for work, I had an amazing feeling of being free. I know I've always been free but, that day, I felt totally aware of it. I can stop for coffee, have a break, get some fresh air – basically, do whatever I like.

I started to get those flashes of freedom, perhaps even of happiness, more and more often. Then, on New Year's Eve 2011, a complete miracle came into my life when I found out that I was pregnant. After being told it would never happen, and desperately trying to pull the money together for IVF, this was the most wonderful thing that could happen to us. I felt complete, and pure happiness washed over me as I looked at the positive pregnancy test. An early scan ruled out any threat of it being ectopic, and I started to feel that maybe, just maybe, everything was fine.

'Perhaps I can actually do this!' I said to Elroy, delirious with the possibility of being a mum again.

'Of course you can, you can do anything,' he told me, grinning with delight.

'Maybe this was life's plan for me all along,' I replied. 'I just needed to wait until I was ready to raise a child free from the terror of perpetrators – just maybe. I couldn't face it before, but maybe now after court and everything, I'm healed enough. Do you think that's what it is?'

He smiled, happy enough to indulge me in whatever reason I came up with, happy to see the pure joy shining from me. I started to look forward, to think I had a fresh start; but sadly, at the three-month scan we discovered that our baby had died. We were devastated. How could life be so cruel? This was my one-in-a-million chance to prove that I could be a healthy, free parent; it felt like life

234

gave me a miracle but then cruelly snatched it away again. I spent two days at home waiting to go into hospital. I still felt pregnant and I was told my body was holding on to the pregnancy. I was finally admitted to Liverpool Women's Hospital, for a six-hour procedure; I ended up being in there for five days as, after five attempts with medication failed, I had to go to theatre.

The next few months were difficult and I felt as though it was me, it was something I'd brought on myself. I wondered if I deserved to be happy. I'd figured that taking Norman to court would be like a magic switch, that I would feel normal for the first time and that it would all be behind me. That the moment of sheer freedom I'd had in the car would be how my life would feel now. I was wrong. Although I was definitely clearer on some things and had closure with Norman, my turmoil continued. It wasn't a magic bullet. I still felt black and foggy and incomplete and unlovable; recovery was a long road.

As time went on, I realised I was struggling to feel emotionally healthy and that there was no magic switch. I still saw Norman everywhere and I still had awful nightmares. In a recurring one I go 'home' to my house, but instead of finding Elroy there, my mother and Norman are waiting. She is always angry and he sits on the sofa, having got out of prison. He's waiting for me and he grins, then follows me to my room and takes his 'revenge' on me for sending him to prison.

235

I'm working out that a lot of things done to me as a child were designed to humiliate me, keep me isolated from people who may have been a support to me, and to destroy my self-esteem. Telling me that my grandparents hated me, that other family members had no time for us and considered me the instigator of our family problems, destroyed any self-confidence in me and made me sure I was a bad person. Mum telling me that Grandma was an abuser and that Grandpa tried to rape her were also surefire ways to make it impossible for me to ever trust them completely. Norman would say, 'If you tell your mum, she'll die. She's too ill for this.'

Even though I've come a long way, I still feel largely unlovable and I wrestle with my rational side and my irrational side. The struggle is still there. If someone seems to like me, I usually feel I have deceived them in some way and that they just can't see the 'real darkness' me just yet. I feel often people 'must' criticise things that I do. I feel that I still grieve for a lost innocence and childhood freedom that is every child's right.

Having said and felt all of this, I know I am recognising wrong thoughts and feelings of 'truth' and starting to challenge them. My determination to feel normal and for closure will overcome all this eventually. I am looking at some things differently now and I recognise the damage done to me by my parents; and it's going to disappear as my truth and become a lie told by bad people. I've been emotionally damaged by people all my life and for it still to be happening – enough is enough. My fight starts here.

When I decided to write this book, I did so for two reasons – I wanted Jenny to finally be acknowledged and I wanted someone else, anyone, to get from it the strength to take their abuser to court. I wanted them to see that it could be done, and that there was hope. After thirty years, without real evidence other than my own voice, my father went to prison for sixteen years.

However, the process has been harder than I could ever have imagined. When you read a book like this, you want it to be straightforward – this happened, then this, then this. And you want a happy ending. I haven't been able to do that, not in any sort of traditional way, because life doesn't work out as easily. I don't have memories from the day I was born – who does? I don't have Jenny to tell me her story. I have had to piece together so much, and my memories are slippery things that, finally, make up no more than a jagged patchwork of my life.

So, the memories all flood in sometimes, they refuse to come at other times, they repeat and they replay. The one about the Michael Jackson poster is there often, I think because it's so bizarre, and I constantly think back to parts of it such as using my dressing gown and coats to cover every inch of the inside of my bedroom door so Norman couldn't spy on me at night. I think about the time Mum put the lock on. I remember being forced into sleeping all night in their bed when she was in hospital, when I was twelve. I remember him taking every single opportunity to get to me, to corner me in the kitchen and put his hands inside my clothes, not stopping even if my brother walked in. The bathroom, any bedroom, the hallways – he followed my every move and I moved around only when I thought it would be 'safe'. That was my life, every day.

I remember him coming into the bathroom, ordering me to lie on the floor. I refused, so he threatened to take all his clothes off so someone would see. I was so scared that I did what he said, confused, wondering whether I should risk the shame of someone seeing but also hopeful that might stop it. I remember him sometimes calling me Netty, my aunt's name, when he was raping me. I remember always having to work out when I could do my many chores, as I couldn't go upstairs to clean if no one else was up there. I had to plan it all out, and he was always getting angry with me for outsmarting him.

Every time I get upset about things – whether inconsequential or not – the other memories rush back; it's as if my mind is looking for an excuse to upset me, never giving me peace. It's as if they're shouting at me, telling me not to forget, telling me that this all matters. I remember, I remember, I remember. I remember being made to polish in their bedroom. As soon as my mother went out, he came straight in, pushed me onto the bed and raised his fist to hit me when I protested. I think he would have battered me senseless if I hadn't let him do what he wanted.

I remember that he held me against the wall on the landing by my throat when I tried to stop him. I remember being scared all the time, with my whole life revolving around avoiding him. I remember going to the toilet only when it was safe, or using a plastic Tupperware bowl in my room because I knew that he was quietly waiting for me to have to leave my room. I felt disgusting, ashamed, frightened. I remember living with a knot in my stomach, afraid to go home. I remember being completely alone.

And that, that is what you live with when you're an abuse survivor. Your mind races with memories all the time, your dreams are filled with terrors. You never know when it will hit you, because it has filled your formative years.

As I finished writing the book, I knew there was one person I had to talk to about it all. I've always been close to my eldest brother, Ian, but I knew he had his own demons. Although I was trying to process mine, and he had said he would be there for me, I did wonder how all of this was affecting him. By telling my story, I was opening up everything about my family, and I knew from the start that there would be repercussions. I desperately hoped Ian and I would still be strong together, still love each other, when this part of that story was over.

We Skyped each other and he told me he would be by my side for as long as I needed him, that he would stand by everything we both knew was true, and that – for the first time ever – he would let me read his witness statement, which he sent through to me. Although Norman was not Ian's biological father, he had been there for most of his childhood – and had left his mark. As I absorbed the words that he had said to the police I realised, yet again, just how much damage had been done to so many people by the toxic pair I called my parents.

The statement reads:

I am the above named person and I live at an address known to Merseyside Police. I make this statement in relation to an allegation of sexual abuse made by my sister Karen Walker against my stepfather Norman Yeo.

Unfortunately, I cannot access most of my childhood memories. I've always believed this was due to something that must have happened when I was a kid because, when I try to, I get very uncomfortable and it is almost like there is a pain in my head.

The following is an account of the few things I am able to access and an overall picture of my stepfather.

Fear. That is what I mostly remember about Norman. Me always being in fear of Norman coming home. I knew I would be getting a beating but didn't know what he would use this time or how severe it would be. I do remember he always knocked my glasses off first and then he would use his hands, fists and other implements such as my cricket bat or the metal soup ladle. I'm told that he would usually pull out clumps of my hair.

On one occasion, when I must have been about 15, he was hitting me and taunting me to hit him back, telling me to 'be a man'. I was a 15 year old, about 5' 4" of scrawniness and he was the fear-inspiring father figure of over 6 foot. That one time, though, I finally tried and was beaten so badly that it has become a blank after me hitting him back.

He never really needed a reason for his beatings and, after growing up, I assumed it was just a problem he had or he hated the fact that I wasn't naturally his. This left me as a timid child who rarely played out unless forced to by my mum.

As a kid I ran away from home twice. Once when I was very young and once as a teen. On the first occasion, I took Jennifer with me and all I remember about it is that we left through the living room window and were in fear of something. The second occasion is a little clearer. Jennifer wasn't living with us but I took Karen and, again, we were in fear of something (presumably Norman). We ended up at the back of an abandoned house and I'm told that

I left a note saying we were going to kill ourselves. Apparently the Police were informed and broadcasts were made on the local radio.

I honestly do not know if I knew what was going on with Karen and Jennifer but it seems I was trying to protect them from something and I do recall that as we were getting older, I noticed Karen becoming more withdrawn and nervous, especially around Norman.

I've often tried to pierce through whatever the block is in my memory and I've wondered if it was sexual abuse for me as well. I've told myself that I don't care if it was, that I care more about the fact that it happened to Karen and Jenny but would just like to know if that was the reason. The only clues I have to it being a possibility (apart from the block itself) are fuzzy memories. One is of being in the bathroom with Norman whilst he was naked in the shower and another where I was, for some reason, showing my naked backside in the living room and Norman and his friend were there. I also recall when, as a teen, I found Norman's stash of pornography. Most of it was the usual girlie magazine stuff except for one magazine, which was all naked men. Needless to say, that stuck in my memory.

My childhood has left me as someone suffering from depression, someone who mostly stays in the house and no longer seeks out relationships, primarily because I always feel like a fraud, that I am play-acting being an adult when really, I'm still a frightened kid. I am able to fool people when I am out because I usually portray confidence and sociability but I can't seem to make those feelings real nor parlay them into a proper relationship with a partner. I don't feel sorry for myself or anything and I know I have to change but it is really difficult to find the motivation. Again, I care more about what happened to my sisters. I've lost Jenny and I think her self-destruction was definitely all about her childhood and what she endured at the hands of Norman. As for Karen, I am constantly amazed and awestruck at what a loving person she still is, despite what she went through. She has her problems too, of course, and they too are due to what she went through as a child and she is working on them. As for my brothers, they too have their demons to work out.

Overall, Norman was a destructive force in our lives. He was often away fishing as he rarely worked and those times were easier and lighter for us but always with the spectre of him returning as that would mean more violence and beatings, crying and punishments whether we had done anything 'wrong' or not.

* * *

Reading that statement hit me hard. So much of this I had never seen before, and it broke my heart to think Ian was pouring it all out now, still trying to help me, still being my big brother. I think mentioning the pornography in his court statement helped the jury believe me, as I'd said it was one of the early grooming tools that Norman had used against me. When he and Mum both denied having it in the house, the jury must have had to decide who to believe – our parents, or Ian and me. I also didn't remember us writing a suicide note when we ran away. I do remember the actual running away with him though, and thinking we would live in a big old abandoned house that we found, but the suicide note was something that had been forgotten, for me, in the mists of time.

When Ian sent me that letter, I asked him if he thought he might regret it being included in the book.

'No,' he replied, without any pause whatsoever. 'I don't care what is used, because it's the truth. If my memories help to give yours credibility, that's only a good thing. As a child, I witnessed those two holding Jenny by each arm, at the top of the stairs, both pulling her in different directions because Lesley was trying to throw her down the stairs. I found the porn, and I was being beaten for it, but I also know Lesley had "books" that were hers, that were nothing to do with Norman. They were beyond vile, they were full of animal porn, people having sex with dogs and donkeys. How sick is that? It made me want to vomit. I think that defending Lesley came from fear – fear that came from knowing what she was really like.'

I get that. I think Ian's protectiveness, which is sometimes very over-the-top, comes from being the oldest sibling and feeling like it was his 'duty'. I've tried to tell him over and over that it wasn't his responsibility, that he was just a little boy and that only two people were responsible, but those deep-rooted feelings won't disappear just because his little sister tells him what she thinks is going on. Writing that testimony for me was such a brave thing to do, because by writing this book, I know I have put it all in the spotlight. Perhaps one day he will tell his story. I hope so.

When my auntie got Nanny's diaries after her death, there was lots in there about Mum – she said she was 'the eternal victim' and she wondered where they had gone wrong to make her turn out the way she did. It was clear that they never knew what to do with her, that they had been at their wits' end about her behaviour ever since she was a little girl. I know Mum kept me away from anyone who could tell me the truth, and that, when Granddad died when I was nine, things got even worse. The food he brought, the money he gave her – that all stopped, and she resented it. She would tell him that the kids were starving and he would always help out when he could; even though she fed herself first and spent the money on her own clothes and make-up, he was there, and sometimes she was calmed down a bit by the fact that she had got something. When he died, that was lost. I don't remember her ever grieving for him, just being angry that one of her easy options had gone.

People call it 'historical' abuse, but there is nothing historical about what I'm living. Every day, there is something to remind me of what was done to me, what he did to me. I know I was lucky to get a conviction, but how sick is that? How appalling is it that we use the word 'lucky' when an abuser gets a tiny portion of what they deserve? He got convicted, but I got a life sentence – and, Jenny, you didn't even get the chance to live your life at all.

I know we need shorthand phrases to try to help people have some understanding, any understanding, of these horrific crimes, but I often feel as if there's more time and effort spent on getting the words right than there is on protecting children or supporting survivors. And there's another one right there – 'survivors'. So many groups and individuals have fought to move away from calling us 'victims' – we are strong, we have got through this, we have survived; but the truth is, sometimes I don't feel like a survivor. I feel guilty even writing that but I do, at times, wonder if there would be more sympathy or understanding if we used the word 'victim'. You don't survive a burglary, you don't survive a mugging; you're seen as a victim, so why, when the most personal thing of all has been attacked and stolen and taken, is there such pressure to label yourself as a survivor? I know the arguments behind it, I know it's meant to be empowering, but there are so many times when I want to scream, *This still affects me, this still hurts, I am still in such a lot of pain and I fear it will never end.*

Whereas other people have warm childhood memories about things like friends and Christmas and birthdays, I don't. Everything is coloured by the people I called my parents. My childhood has so little to make me smile; it doesn't even have much in the way of difference from day to day, week to week, month to month, year to year. I wonder if, without those files, I would even have any structure to my memories. I get small flashes, but very little that brings back a full story. So I recall the pretend house from when I started school that I mentioned at the start of the book. But then the sadness comes in as I remember I was overjoyed just to be playing, at everyone smiling around me, and how unusual that was. I remember Ian and I used to walk to and from school alone between the ages of five and eight, but all I can wonder is, did no one walk with him before? Was he all alone?

When I was seven and moved to another primary school, on my very first day I went to the wrong toilets, a big brick outhouse at the end of the schoolyard. The teacher seemed cross with me, as though I had done it on purpose. I know that back then I already felt 'not good enough'. I was just not as good as the other children. I was 'dilatory'. The only time I was happy then was when I found a blue Snoopy watch at school – his arms were the watch hands! – and I was allowed to keep it as no one said it was theirs. I loved it and treasured it for years.

At middle school, I did like music, but my time was made terrible through being bullied by the 'popular' kids, who called me scruffy. I felt like an outsider and that I was a bad person inside. The abuse was daily by that time, but I never said anything to anyone. I thought everyone did it, I really did.

There are a few good memories about high school, and I did make some friends there – I even liked the 'nit nurse'! Jenny and I would walk to this school together when she was staying at home; we would steal bread from our kitchen to eat on the way as Jenny was usually hungry from having no tea.

I did OK, I suppose, given what I was enduring at home. I enjoyed English, Biology and Home Economics, but P.E. was quite difficult for me as I was so body conscious and often didn't have nice underwear or the correct clothes to wear. I was embarrassed, so I would make up excuses to get out of PE, and could never go swimming as I didn't have a costume. I couldn't say that, so I made up a problem each time and got into trouble a lot. I could never go on school outings or trips as my parents wouldn't pay the small surcharge that parents on low incomes had to pay; another reason for me to get into trouble, as I lied a few times and said I'd lost the money.

I was known at school as 'quiet little Karen' and left with eight CSE passes, but what really sticks with me as I reflect on all those years was that there were no knights in shining armour: no teachers to rescue me, nobody to notice the quiet little girl with the sad eyes. Nobody noticed anything, with me or with Jenny. They were all oblivious. Even when I became a mother, no one picked up on anything.

There is no doubt that I had issues with my parenting – I hated to leave Karl with anyone because I just couldn't believe he would be safe. I didn't want anyone to bathe him or change his nappy and I knew, while he was still quite young, that I would only ever be able to have one child because I worried so much about having any more, especially little girls. I was scared about what my own reaction would be if they were ever around men. Would I panic? Would I see things that weren't there? Would I see things if they *were* there? Knowing that, even now, I have suspicious thoughts when I see men with children and something seems 'off', I don't think I could ever have coped with more than one child; I would have been too scared that I was taking my eye off the ball with one while I paid attention to the other.

I can't help these things. They haunt me, and that's why

I often think of myself as a victim, not a survivor. And then there's you, Jenny: you have to be a victim because you were never given the chance to survive, were you?

I try to live by the motto, 'Always have a backup plan' because I believe that is the key to a successful life that flows through the ups and downs. You never know what is round the corner – in fact, not knowing what's next is the only thing you can rely on! Everyone in my life knows me for saying, 'Keep smiling', because I really do feel that you have to – you have to keep pushing through. I've been given so many gifts with this phrase on over the years – cups, wall plaques and such – and I will try to stick to the feeling that a smile makes everything better until my last breath.

Is my heart broken? Yes, yes it is, but I like to think of a broken heart very much as a cut or piece of broken skin . . . at first it bleeds so much and hurts with such intensity that you can't bear it. You cover it with plasters to try to stop the bleeding and pain, much like the bargaining, denial and anger we feel after losing a loved one. Eventually, the cut knits together and the pain eases, but it's still there, every day. Some day, some time afterwards, you might realise it doesn't hurt at all; but if you press your finger on the scar (or go to your memories) it hurts again. The scar (the loss) never really goes away as we have a permanent reminder – on our skin or in our heart – but we learn to live with it.

I try to tell the younger people in my life to go out there, take chances, fail, pick themselves up again, go and look at the world, move around, see everything; nothing is set in stone and there is always another way (the 'backup plan'). The saddest thing in life, in my opinion, is to stay in one place. The time may never seem just right, but you have to go for it – sometimes you have to take a leap from that mountain and trust in your own wings.

I've undertaken CBT training and life coach qualifications, which means I've picked up a lot of wisdom and had a lot of light-bulb moments, and a few of these are worth passing on, I hope. Sometimes, when talking to people who are very down on themselves due to getting older, I remind them that they're never going to be this young again, and this always makes people smile. When I have been with a person who feels their life is done (at fifty or sixty years old!), I sometimes feel I have my work cut out, but it can still be done.

I have had family members and friends complain that they're 'past it', or their joints hurt, or that they have done their bit, they're too old, they've had their life. I always say to them, 'Put yourself twenty years from now and look back at the person you are today – what are you saying to today's you? Are you saying "Wow, I was just a lad or lass then, and I still had the world at my feet? I still had my health. I wish I had done those things

I wanted to do."?' This is very powerful and people tend to realise the truth of that maybe for the first time.

I like to tell people – in life, if you get a NO, see it as an acronym for Next One! I ask people if they have a goal in life, and they tend to list them. I then ask them which ones they are actively taking steps towards achieving. They usually answer 'None', to which I reply 'So you have dreams, nice ideas for your life, not goals; goals are something you are actively moving towards.'

Another thing I like to tell people is that there are no failures in their life, only lessons, only steps. I use the light-bulb example – Thomas Edison was asked how it felt to have failed 1,000 times while inventing the light bulb. He said, 'I didn't fail a thousand times, the light bulb took a thousand attempts to perfect.' It's true! We can only progress through making mistakes and learning from them. I always like to remember the saying, 'Whether you believe you can or you believe you can't, you are probably right.' And I've believed I can do this for a while now – I really have.

Writing all of this down, writing it all to you, has brought it into such clear relief – I thought I had learned to live with it and handle it, but I know that I struggle at times. The feelings of worthlessness, low self-esteem and self-hatred last a lifetime, but do you know what, Jenny? I think I'm finally there, I think I'm finally ready to step out

252

into the light and say, I made it. You didn't break me. I'm still here, I'm still standing and I am shouting loud enough for both of us. Sisters, for ever, despite what they tried to do.

EPILOGUE

After the conviction, I was faced with yet another wave of official records, this time in the form of newspaper reports, which again laid out the details of my life in such a basic, brutal manner:

> He pleaded guilty to indecently assaulting his victim between the ages of 11 years old and 16 years old and was found guilty of rape and indecently assaulting his victim between the ages of 8 years old and 16 years old. The sexual offences began in 1979, and the rape convictions reflect a course of conduct from when the victim was 8 years old to 16 years old.
>
> The judge said: 'This case concerns regular, repeated, systematic sexual abuse ... You are disgusted with yourself ... and so you should be.'

Judge John Phipps told him that he had 'ruined' his victim's childhood and his abuse had affected her entire life as he jailed him for 16 years. [. . .] Judge Phipps told Yeo, who showed no emotion, that he had 'secured the child's silence, initially by telling her it was normal behaviour and later by subtle pressure'.

Some published reports totalled twenty-three counts but it was definitely twenty-four. Maybe someone got their sums wrong, or printed a typo. Either way, I cannot change what's printed by others but I do know the number off by heart. Twenty-four, twenty-four, twenty-four – it's burned into my memory.

But I wondered, was Norman actually disgusted by what he did? Certainly not enough to tell the truth or admit the full scale of it when forced to go to court. After all, he denied raping me, he claimed the abuse 'only' began after I turned eleven – as if that made it acceptable – and his denials meant that I had to relive it all.

The newspaper articles show an old man with a gaping mouth, a look of confusion and a lacerated face. The reason for the cuts on his face was actually that he had fallen while he was drunk, but it did give him a look of vulnerability, as if this poor old soul had been beaten by fellow prisoners when they discovered his crime. I hated those pictures. I hated to see him. I hated to read his name.

I couldn't stop reading it, though. Jenny – I couldn't

stop looking at what had been printed. Yes, there was some sort of reckoning there, but he had got away with so much. You had been painted out of the picture, and the version everyone knew was actually pretty sanitised, even though they all said it was horrific.

There's a saying I love: 'You didn't get this far to only get this far' – and I couldn't get it out of my mind. I was proud of what I had done, what *we* had done, but the floodgates were well and truly open this time. I couldn't stop the memories, the flashbacks, the constant film reel in my head showing the same horror story over and over again. I woke up one morning and found a piece of A4 paper in my bed, at the side of me, and I couldn't even remember writing the things that were on it. The sheet was folded in half, like a book, and, on it were twenty-six points that must have come to me when I was falling in and out of sleep, in and out of awareness but always, always, always, with all of this bubbling away, filling my subconscious, remarks from the files, all the horrible detail of my sister's life.

1. Jenny was found tied to a cot at 2.30pm in the afternoon at the age of two – hadn't been fed since lunchtime the day before.
2. Jenny spent lunch and tea at home, having one boiled egg, but got huge dinner from social worker later on.

3. Terrified of bathtubs/bathrooms/complained of being hit and locked in the bathroom.

4. At the age of two or three, her head was flushed down the toilet.

5. She asked the social worker if she would be her mummy.

6. She was covered head to toe in bruises and there were photos.

7. She was taken to A&E on suspicion of a fractured skull.

8. She was first taken away at eighteen months, all of us were at some point, Jenny battered when she was.

9. Dad admitted she was never wanted and Mum said at one point that she 'looked like her dad'.

10. They never visited or wrote to or telephoned the children's home.

11. Social workers wrote so much about them – Mrs Yeo in one of her moods; Mrs Yeo verbally abusive to all children; Mr and Mrs Yeo show no emotion or feelings to these children; children lived in substandard manner, never had an outing or holiday or even a day trip; Mrs Yeo manipulates people and the system, only wants Jenny back for her pride and to get us off her back; Mr Yeo took Jenny to live with his mother, for her safety, and admitted his wife

was violent, doesn't want her and does beat her.

12. Karen and brother – bruises on head.
13. Karen and brother – taken to doctors with cut mouths but refused to open door to social workers.
14. Karen showing signs like Jenny – was verbally abused when social workers arrived at door, she kept her eyes constantly on her mum at age three until she fell asleep on couch.
15. Mr and Mrs Yeo never ask about Jenny on home visits.
16. Mr and Mrs Yeo in a destructive relationship, constant physical abuse, she tells of his insatiable sex drive.
17. Visit to house at 11.30am – only children up.
18. Mr Yeo only looks for a job in the afternoons as he fishes in the morning.
19. Mr and Mrs Yeo asked over and over to visit Jenny – same old excuses, no money, no babysitters, excuses!!
20. Mrs Yeo said, why should I bother to visit her when you won't let her come home until she's eighteen?
21. Social worker wanted to take Ian on a day trip – parents only had to contribute £5; under duress they gave £2.
22. Social workers took children on a day trip, all very excitable as first day out ever.

23. Jenny gained weight as soon as she went into care home.
24. Mrs Yeo in one of her moods today – very aggressive.
25. Mrs Yeo happy today – makes a nice change, all in a good mood.
26. Mrs Yeo says Jenny was a difficult child from conception!

I was stunned to see the information that my mind had decided was the most important. I wanted to make something of it, to remember each and every point, and I did try. I repeated them all; I tried to make a mind tattoo of all the things that had been done, before finally realising . . . it didn't matter.

The past was just that – the past.

I love you with all my heart, Jenny. I do still cry, of course I do, because I miss you and I grieve for the life you never had. But, finally, I am proud of us. You gave me the strength to do this and that's huge. I feel that I am finally in a place where I don't hate the blood that runs through my veins – I cherish it because I share some of it with you.

When the verdict came in, I took a flask of tea to your graveside and told you what had happened. You'd always loved a cup of tea, and it was one of the tiny things I could do to feel close to you. 'He's going to jail, Jenny,' I whispered, even though there was no one nearby.

260

'Norman is going to jail – he's finally having to face up to what he's done. I couldn't have done it without you,' I told her. 'I feel as if you were there every step of the way.'

And then, I just started weeping as if it would never end. All of the emotion, all of the pain, came out there at her graveside, and I began to shake. I knew it was something else too, though; I felt that, somehow, part of our journey together was ending. I held my mug of tea up to Jenny's grave, whispered 'Goodbye' and walked away, the tears still stinging my eyes and chilling my cheeks.

I knew I had to move on. I couldn't let this colour the rest of my life or he would have won. Now, writing this, I feel my destiny has been fulfilled. I am here to tell your story and that's what matters to me. Donna has gone on to make a life for herself with her daughter. She's a good girl with a good heart, like her mum. As I, hopefully, live my life for both of us, coaching and counselling others, being a mother, wife and grandmother, I will do it for you too. I will live twice as hard, love twice as hard and never, ever forget you, my darling big sister.

And please, for anyone who is reading this and has been touched by our story, may I just ask you to remember one thing?

Her name was Jenny xx

ACKNOWLEDGEMENTS

There are so many people to thank – Elroy, my partner, for always standing by me, loving me when I am not very lovable and listening to me for hours on end. For being the broad shoulders I have needed so many times, and for always being truthful with me even when I didn't really want the truth.

Karl, my son – for teaching me what it is to love.

My best friend, Gail – without you, I would not be the woman I am today. You give me unconditional love and strength, and always have my back.

Kerry, my friend – you get me like no other, you hold me up or make me laugh, whichever I need.

Nicky – my honorary sister. We have been through a lot and you have always been by my side, with love and support.

Vicky from the abuse survivors' support group – you are an angel. You got me through the toughest year of my life and you hold a special place in my heart.

Linda Watson-Brown, my ghostwriter – you have supported me and showed me that I am worthy, and you never gave up on me, waiting until the time was right for us to do this.

Ciara and everyone at John Blake Publishing – for giving me this chance to share my story, to give my sister and me a voice and hopefully to help other abuse survivors to find their own voice.

Winston, my gorgeous, big, soft, adorable dog, who has brought such happiness into my life and who has made me realise just how much animals can bring to our world when we give them the unconditional love they offer us. I won't forget all those other poor creatures who were brought into our childhood and then discarded just as quickly, but Winston has mended my heart just a little.